Building a Data Integration Team

Skills, Requirements, and Solutions for Designing Integrations

Jarrett Goldfedder

Apress®

Building a Data Integration Team: Skills, Requirements, and Solutions for Designing Integrations

Jarrett Goldfedder
Vienna, VA, USA

ISBN-13 (pbk): 978-1-4842-5652-7   ISBN-13 (electronic): 978-1-4842-5653-4
https://doi.org/10.1007/978-1-4842-5653-4

Managing Director, Apress Media LLC: Welmoed Spahr
Acquisitions Editor: Susan McDermott
Development Editor: Laura Berendson
Coordinating Editor: Jessica Vakili

Distributed to the book trade worldwide by Springer Science+Business Media New York, 233 Spring Street, 6th Floor, New York, NY 10013. Phone 1-800-SPRINGER, fax (201) 348-4505, e-mail orders-ny@springer-sbm.com, or visit www.springeronline.com. Apress Media, LLC is a California LLC and the sole member (owner) is Springer Science + Business Media Finance Inc (SSBM Finance Inc). SSBM Finance Inc is a **Delaware** corporation.

For information on translations, please e-mail rights@apress.com, or visit http://www.apress.com/rights-permissions.

Apress titles may be purchased in bulk for academic, corporate, or promotional use. eBook versions and licenses are also available for most titles. For more information, reference our Print and eBook Bulk Sales web page at http://www.apress.com/bulk-sales.

Any source code or other supplementary material referenced by the author in this book is available to readers on GitHub via the book's product page, located at www.apress.com/978-1-4842-5652-7. For more detailed information, please visit http://www.apress.com/source-code.

Printed on acid-free paper

To Heather and Melinda

I could not have wished for better people on this journey.

Table of Contents

About the Author

Jarrett Goldfedder is the founder of InfoThoughts Data, LLC, a company that specializes in data management, migration, and automation. He has significant experience in both cloud-based and on-premise technologies and holds various certificates in Salesforce Administration, Dell Boomi Architecture, and Informatica Cloud Data. He also served as a technical reviewer of the Apress book by David Masri titled *Developing Data Migrations and Integrations with Salesforce: Patterns and Best Practices.*

About the Technical Reviewer

Wendy Zhou is a data visualization pioneer in ASB Bank who is passionate about leveraging data and emerging technology to tell fascinating stories. She tailors and facilitates Tableau training for her clients and colleagues, in a way that everyone can enjoy the peace and love of data with less drama.

She is a client-centric strategist with the heart of a revolutionary artist. She has been traveling with her young family while simultaneously working and solving data world problems for her clients from government to healthcare and Fortune 500 to rocket start-ups in Canada, New Zealand, and China.

She has a giving heart and has served as a TUG leader in Montreal, Canada, and Auckland, New Zealand, from 2013 to 2016.

She is the mother of three beautiful children and lives in the land of the long white cloud, New Zealand. She loves cooking (but not baking!). She is also a YouTube-taught hairdresser (check out her FB page, Wendy's Barbershop) and enjoys many activities from crocheting to violin playing.

Acknowledgments

I wrote this book for many reasons, but primarily so that data teams could have a handy reference and guide when their integration projects inevitably slip off the rails. As I will mention over and over, it is no fun to find ourselves with too little time and too many deliverables, rushing headlong into panic mode while the hours ebb deep into the night. Trial and error no doubt plays a huge role in figuring out how to get out of the mess we've either created or inherited, and I assure you, I've been there. With that in mind, several people have been instrumental in supporting me as well as finding the right solutions and principles summarized in this book.

To my parents, Arthur and Lila Goldfedder: Ever since I was a child, I said I wanted to be a writer. Finally, we have something to put on that empty bookshelf. Thank you for all you've done to motivate me and give me a sense of joy and pride. I hope this book does the same for you.

To my brother, Brandon Goldfedder: Without a doubt, everything I know about computers is because of you. I am proud to have you as a brother and an even better friend that carefully listened as I complained about writing for 3 hours with only two pages to show for it. Yes, you're right: pictures help.

To the team at Acumen Solutions: A big shout-out to Cristina Miller, Adam Horvath, Saurabh Verma, and Chuck Boyd who coached me while I worked at Acumen. You allowed me the space to discuss, test, experiment, lament, and brainstorm many ideas, some good and some not as good. It was through your open-mindedness, patience, and commitment that I acquired the experience to write this book. I am very grateful.

To the team at Apress, Jessica Vakili, Susan McDermott, and Laura Berendson: A thousand thank-yous for believing in me when I made the pitch for this book and for checking in to make sure it all went like clockwork. You are my go-tos for the next time around.

ACKNOWLEDGMENTS

To my technical reviewer, Wendy Zhou: You became the first deep-dive reviewer of this book. Your comments and feedback significantly boosted my confidence when I stumbled over the question just about every technical writer faces: "What if no one understands this?" You assured me they would, and while I can't guarantee initial reactions, at least I know that I'm not alone with the problem that we are trying to solve, and you made it all worth it.

To my wife and daughter, Heather and Melinda, to whom this book is dedicated: Thank you for giving me the time and space I needed, even when it meant weekends in seclusion, and exciting you both by talking about the latest trends in data integration after your long days of work and school. You two are the best. Me more.

Introduction

Without a systematic way to start and keep data clean, bad data will happen.

—Donato Diorio, CEO of RingLead[1]

My Story

I was just out of school and relatively new to the world of data integration when I received my first hard lesson about project management: "Nothing is ever as easy as the Statement of Work (SOW) claims it will be." In this case, I was part of a five-person consulting team building a web application. Our roles were clearly defined: one project manager (PM), one business analyst (BA), two web developers, and one data integration specialist. I was the data integration specialist, and I was proud of that title, albeit I didn't know much about what I would be doing. Nor did I know that as the new guy, I was expendable. This project would be a trial by fire experience since data integration was a relatively new service offered by the company, and they realized they had nothing to lose by throwing me straight into the fire.

My main goals, according to the two pages provided in the otherwise bulky, hardbound Statement of Work, would be to import around 15,000 addresses from an Excel spreadsheet into a SQL Server 7.0 database. In other words, our customers would be providing us all the fields we needed. I had three basic tasks (see Figure 1):

1. Create the associated tables and fields in the SQL Server database.

2. Import the addresses from the spreadsheet.

3. Ensure that the 15,000 records match between the Excel spreadsheet and the database.

---

[1]Lisa Lee, Kim Honjo, and Samantha Steiny. 2019. "20 Inspirational Quotes About Data." *Salesforce Blog.* www.salesforce.com/blog/2014/07/data-quotes-gp.html

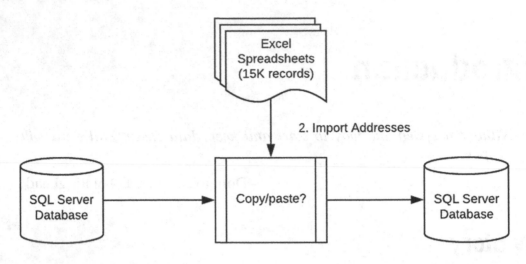

Figure 1. *My First Integration (Surface View)*

Yes, it looked pretty simple on paper, even for someone like me, whose most complicated integration to date was copying and pasting undergrad Psych 101 grades from Notepad into a Lotus database. Still, it was so simple that when our developers realized that our web application required a bit more tweaking before going into Production, I did not worry. Yes, it was a blocker, but we still had plenty of time. Heck, if worse came to worse, I could always perform the unimaginable and work late on a Friday night (remember, I was brand new at this consulting thing). As long as we had the sample data loaded by our due date, it would all work out. It was a copy/paste, but with maybe a few more buttons to push.

Creating the table and fields in SQL Server was easy. Getting the import file was not. It finally arrived on a USB drive by Thursday morning. Loading it, I gradually realized there was a problem. The fields themselves looked, well, unusual. Through some strange comma-delimited gymnastics, what should have been State was hanging out in the Country field. We had empty phone numbers, some that were just "0" (were we calling the operator?), and even human-accepted values like "N/A" which would have choked when being read into a numeric open table field. After some hesitation, I finally had to admit that I could not work with this data.

Step 2 started after spending most of Thursday and Friday working with our client to manually clean up the 15,000 records. It was now time to import the addresses from the spreadsheet, which should have been just a copy/paste between Window applications.

In reality, it involved much, much more (see Figure 2). First, the proprietary driver of Excel had not been installed correctly in the database, and I immediately received a "File not found" error. Okay, a slight miscommunication there, but quickly resolved if I just exported the Excel file into a new comma-delimited file.

Well, not really. The import worked fine unless the contact just happened to have a postal code in any town from New Jersey, Massachusetts, or any other state where the US Postal Zip Code starts with a zero ("0"). Excel has an interesting feature where, if not correctly defined as a format, fields beginning with "0s" are removed on export automatically (we refer to this as a "leading zero," and you can read more about a workaround here—*https://support.office.com/en-us/article/format-numbers-to-keep-leading-zeros-in-excel-online-633401e5-f2ad-4ac7-afef-05ed58b1c9a1*).[2] Thus, during our import of 15,000 records, we hit an INVALID LENGTH error on ZIPCODE almost immediately. We were expecting at least five characters, and in this case, we received four. So I would troubleshoot the error, fix it, and start over from scratch until the next field error. And the next, and the next, and so on.

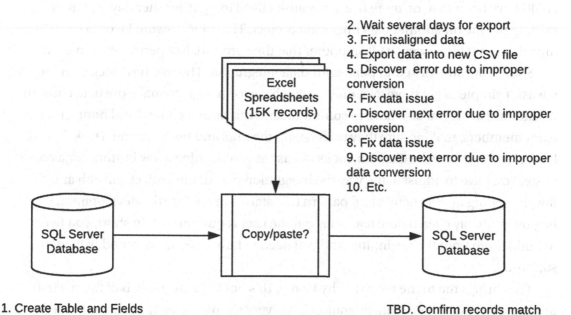

2. Wait several days for export
3. Fix misaligned data
4. Export data into new CSV file
5. Discover error due to improper conversion
6. Fix data issue
7. Discover next error due to improper conversion
8. Fix data issue
9. Discover next error due to improper data conversion
10. Etc.

Excel Spreadsheets (15K records)

SQL Server Database

Copy/paste?

SQL Server Database

1. Create Table and Fields

TBD. Confirm records match

Figure 2. *My First Integration (Actual View)*

[2]"Format Numbers to Keep Leading Zeros in Excel for the Web." 2019. *Support.office.com.* https://support.office.com/en-us/article/format-numbers-to-keep-leading-zeros-in-excel-online-633401e5-f2ad-4ac7-afef-05ed58b1c9a1

It didn't stop there. The path of transforming the data during that long weekend was endless. I learned more than enough hard lessons about migrations (enough to fill a book, cough cough). There were so many aspects to consider, so many things taken for granted that I could have done differently had I only known better. But as the old expression goes: "Turn your wounds into wisdom." I'll keep it at that for now.

I left that experience feeling stunned and exhausted. I dreaded the conversation with the team that followed. I began with "We couldn't deploy because I wasn't ready with the data..."

I will take the position that although my data load was less than stellar, there was some progress made. That's bound to happen with two hours of sleep a night for three nights. But if I take everything into account, the project itself was not a huge success, and only a portion of that was related to the data problems. To my surprise, no one tossed around blame or ever stated the obvious: I was way, way, way over my head as a data integrator.

On the contrary, my manager praised my performance due to my persistence. It could have been that, or, more likely, because I lived to fight another day. In any case, staffing put me on another data migration project. This time, I swore I would learn from my mistakes. Things went a bit smoother that time around. Not perfect, but smoother.

Soon, I became the go-to person for data integration. The role has stuck with me. But it wasn't simple to get there. Not only do you have to struggle to make the data conform to standards, but you also have to communicate with both technical and nontechnical team members, making sure they understand the nuts and bolts around a task that, at least on an architecture diagram, looks as easy as just pushing a few buttons for a copy/ paste. You have to adjust to the way the integration part of the project will ebb and flow by setting up a structure and pattern that starts long before the development work begins, probably even before teams lay out the user requirements. In short, you need to build there from the beginning, and you need to have a team ready and willing to support.

That brings me to the reasons why I wrote this book. There are two of them. First, as I hope I've illustrated, data migration looks very simple, given that you only need to move data from point A to point B, but it can turn quite messy very fast and without warning. The typical results of bad planning are missed deadlines, unrecognized overhead, and, more often than not, desperate acts of last-minute heroism that take on a weirdly optimistic tone ("I did it and with only three hours of sleep in the last two days!").

Of course, I think we would all prefer to do without these results, and I hope this book will help you to plan and coordinate the integration team effort from the outset.

The second reason for writing this book is to emphasize to all parties involved in a project, from the project manager to the developers to the stakeholders, that data migration is one of the most, if not *the* most, critical parts of the project plan. Too often have I seen a migration plan relegated to the back end of the development phase, almost serving as an afterthought to the working piece of software that takes center stage. I argue that this is a mistake because no matter how shiny a software product is, no matter how many features and specifications you add, if the data is not correct—for example, if your bottom-line receipts are missing or your customer data is corrupt—then the software is broken. Period.

Do the migration early and do it right, however, and you'll find there's no greater satisfaction than having clients tell you how much easier their lives have become due to data issues no longer existing. Yes, it can be hard work and long hours in the beginning, but truly worthwhile in the end.

Before we get started on the major topics, let's clear up one misconception right off the bat since I use the terms interchangeably throughout this book. Let's discuss the difference between data migration and data integration.

The Difference Between Data Migration and Data Integration

We define migration as "the movement from one place to another."[3] What immediately may come to mind are antelopes and giraffes traversing from one region of the Serengeti to the next or monarch butterflies drifting south while salmon swim upstream, back to their birthplaces. In the context of data, it is somewhat similar. We are talking about information moving from one server (the origin, or *source*) to another (the destination, or *target*). Migration typically happens once or twice in the lifetime of a particular database product, such as when moving from a legacy database to a more modern practical application.

---

[3]"Migrate"—dictionary definition. 2019. *Vocabulary.com*. www.vocabulary.com/dictionary/migrate

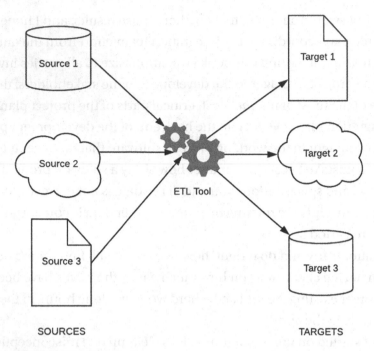

SOURCES   TARGETS

Figure 3. *The Integration Model*

As shown in Figure 3, the migration is not limited just to databases. Excel
spreadsheets, for example, can serve as the source or target systems, and at some point,
maybe after a few months of manually inputting Human Resources (HR) questionnaire
survey results, we would want to move the data to a more efficient storage mechanism.
This move could happen at one time over a weekend (called a "big bang" in some
organizations) or across multiple weekends, weeks, or months (called a delta migration).
The point is that the data does not exist in the target, a migration happens, and then the
data is available for consumption.

Integration, on the other hand, is defined as "the act of combining into an integral
whole."[4] Technically, it means adding or updating new data against *already* existing data.
In other words, data integration is bringing in new or updated data only after an initial
load is complete and systems are operational. The term applies mostly to the data loads
that arrive at odd hours in the early morning, throughout the day, or even moment by
moment (this is sometimes called "real time" or, as purists would prefer, "near-real time"
since there's a slight processing lag between source input and target output).

---

[4]"Integration"—dictionary definition. 2019. *Vocabulary.com*. www.vocabulary.com/dictionary/
 integration

It's essential in a project plan to differentiate between data migration and data integration because the former generally takes much more time to plan and produce than the latter. Data migration requires a complete analysis of the system architecture, data stores, and business requirements, while data integration is usually against an existing system where the explicit instructions and documents already are provided (at least, in theory). Thus, the time to discover and develop a data load is generally quicker in an integration project, although it still has its unique characteristics. Project teams often blur the lines of the two categories together, with the assumption that a more complex data migration approach is just as simple as a plug-and-play data integration would be. As I mentioned earlier, it is a big surprise when the reality sets in, particularly in those cases where migration and integration components haphazardly are consolidated into a single operation within the SOW.

With that difference in mind, this book's title starts with *Building a Data Integration Team*. I could just as quickly have named it *Building a Data Migration Team* or, more accurately, *Building a Data Migration and Data Integration Team*. In the world of migrations, "integration" is often the de facto term used to describe both operations. Most job requisitions seek an "integration engineer" to fill a role and not a "migration engineer." I guess the first phrase is shorter and rolls off the tongue a bit better. Most people—even those who recognize the difference between the two activities—assume that this role will require the ability to migrate as well as build integration processes.

I cover both migration and integration as they require different methodologies, but I will use the term "data integration" to mean both migrations and integrations. By the end of this book, my goal is for you to have knowledge of both topics and be well aware of the nuances between them.

Technical Details: Why Bother?

At this point, you may be wondering why I am bothering you with all the technical details. After all, most realistic projects constrain the number of records required to migrate. Very few of them have millions, and some have even less than the 15,000 that I had to face early in my career. If your project has only a few hundred or so and you're just starting with a brand-new application, wouldn't it be simpler just to insert the data and move ahead?

My response to that is a strong *yes*. In this case, the easiest solution is probably the best. If you can avoid having to implement a detailed data migration project, you probably should. I have defended this position many times in the past by explaining that manually entering data across the scope of a week is probably better than trying to code a complete source-to-target solution that involves methodologies and rules and all the other artifacts that come with project delivery. This clarification often delights the customer looking for a quick turnaround, frustrates the account executive team who sets the fees, and confuses project managers who suddenly must shift their focus away from the integration details and back to software development.

The problem with migrations, as I discussed earlier, is not the easy solution, but the one that only appears to be easy; these situations have much more going on under the surface. Sure, it may be "only" a few hundred records, but how many columns? 5? 10? 100? The more data, the more complexity will be involved. And what about the data structure? Do these columns store easily represented fields like salutation, first name, and last name, or are they large strings like project codes, lengthy IDs, or binary attachments like PDFs that are next to impossible to enter by hand? Even with the best design strategies, there may be one or two "gotchas" that come up to the surface only after teams review the source. For this reason, it is crucial that no matter how simple a migration project may seem, be sure to analyze it as your initial impressions may not be correct. Do this as soon as you can because the moment the project begins, expectations are already set.

Reader Requirements

Now that we know the difference between data migrations and integrations and why considering them matters even for the simplest of projects, it is time for us to talk about what you, the reader, must bring to the table. You're reading this book for a reason—perhaps to learn more about how to build data integration teams, to learn about configuring the right processes, or maybe to acquire a bit more knowledge to share with your existing team. All of these are valid, but they do require you to understand a few things related to the technology we will be discussing.

First, this is not a how-to book on programming, database development, or service-oriented architecture. Although we discuss connecting to remote systems, transforming data, and software that can support migration and integration, I avoid software tutorials, choosing instead to focus on the process. Therefore, being familiar with the underlying technologies will help you follow throughout each chapter.

Second, one of the central tenets for building a successful integration team is strong communication and collaboration—both within and outside the organization. Working with others through discussion, negotiation, and compromise, possessing a basic understanding of workflows (i.e., the lifecycle of a piece of work), and understanding how to hand off work related to your project will help you much more effectively achieve your goal of establishing a highly functioning integration team and framework.

Finally, the number of deliverables for designing and deploying a data migration and integration project can be extensive. For example, not only do you have the business requirements of the entire project to contend with but you also need to tend to your internal designs—system, coding, database, and so on—and that could take hours or even days to prepare and configure. Thus, writing and maintaining documentation is key, and especially knowing the proper usage of requirements documents, sequence diagrams, and flowcharts will aid in getting your message across to everyone who needs to know how your project has progressed and where it is going next.

Chapter Summary

With those requirements in place, we're finally ready to start our journey. Although I recommend reading from cover to cover in order, you can also skip around to find a topic of interest. It's up to you how you want to handle it. For your convenience, I have organized the chapters as follows:

- Chapter 1: Integration Background

  We start with a brief history of data migration, from its earliest days to the modern times of on-premise and ground-to-cloud approaches. We then discuss how migration is more of a process rather than a product and how "owning a process" requires a different perspective than the more familiar "owning a product" that software development entails. We end the chapter with a discussion of integration approaches ranging from the one-time migration to nightly integration, listener services, and hybrid approach.

- Chapter 2: Key Terms

  Integration developed from a combination of both technical and business mind-sets consequently has several terms that require some understanding. This chapter clarifies what these terms mean and why they matter in the integration process.

- Chapter 3: Team Qualifications

  The integration team consists of individuals who are technical engineers, business-focused analysts, great communicators, and experienced coders. While some integration teams are quite small, others can be much larger. This chapter discusses the roles and responsibilities required to create an optimal group.

- Chapter 4: Finding Your Purpose: Project Deliverables

  With a team structure firmly in mind, the next step is to determine what type of functional, business, and technical requirements should be captured and documented. Data integrations tend to be very fluid, and often, mappings can change multiple times before the stakeholders provide final signoff. If large datasets reveal inexplicable errors, developers must quickly research, code, and communicate workarounds to stakeholders. The best way to do this is through a combination of reasonable business requirements, an understanding of who can support change requests, and the right documents to communicate the integration approach.

- Chapter 5: Choosing an ETL Tool

  Depending on the type of integration required, developers and architects need to have experience with database services, cloud platforms, XML, and underlying communication protocols like REST and SOAP. Tying these technologies together requires the right extraction, transformation, and loading (ETL) tool. This chapter discusses how ETL typically operates and includes a sample script to demonstrate the steps to build a simple service. We then go through the current ETL software leaders in the marketplace ranging from the least amount of experience (but with little flexibility) to the more advanced (but with plenty of features). Our goal is to establish the right tool for the right job without having to learn a series of new technologies overnight.

- Chapter 6: A Sample ETL Project

We're now ready to take a break and to start practicing what we've learned. In this chapter, we'll play the role of an integration team and move contact and product data from a source to a target system. We'll review the steps from our previous chapters, design the documents we need, and write code.

- Chapter 7: Platform Automation

One of the hallmarks of a good integration design is that it should be repeatable. The initial load scripts should be tested rigorously on Development and Test environments, and daily processes should run continuously on Production environments, changing where needed to fit the growing needs of the business. Much of this approach relates directly to a development operations (DevOps) model and bears discussing it as it relates to data integration.

- Chapter 8: Monitoring Results

The design is complete, the business is satisfied with the requirements, and the project has gone live. The only thing left to do is to start monitoring the results of the integration. In this chapter, we implement a PDCA (Plan-Do-Check-Act) cycle to improve the integration output, providing daily success and error counts to users through emails and other notification channels. We discuss ways to identify errors, making sure the owners of the data systems know how to resolve their issues once discovered. We end with a brief discussion on using the integration as a feeder into business intelligence, potentially using analytics to find gaps in the data that can lead to additional integration projects.

- Chapter 9: Marketing Your Team

  By this point, the integration team should have deployed at least a few projects and have earned accolades for their successful accomplishments. This celebration is no time to rest on their laurels, however. Before the excitement dies down, teams should reach out to departments across the enterprise, identifying future projects that make the best candidates for data integration. Part of this approach will involve advertising to make external teams aware of the work the integration team has done, performing educational activities such as lunch and learns, and becoming involved with building an integration center of excellence. Understanding the goals of the enterprise for the upcoming fiscal year would also have value; with some research and creativity, the team can construct an integration data roadmap. This visual summary, equivalent to a product roadmap, maps out the vision and direction of integration offerings, which departments they serve, and the estimated time it would take to complete.

CHAPTER 1

Integration Background

If you can't describe what you are doing as a process, you don't know what you're doing.

—W. Edwards Deming[1]

Technology has progressed so quickly in the past few decades that we often forget that what today seems so simple was once quite complex. Data integration first appeared in the 1970s when company personnel recognized that they could use mainframe databases to store different types of business information. Companies and their developers produced early versions of what would become extraction, transformation, and loading (ETL) tools to copy data from one or more sources into destination systems. This housing of these multiple data repositories was the forerunner of today's data warehouses.

During the late 1980s and early 1990s, as the concept of the data warehouse became entwined in mainstream technology, integration between mainframes, minicomputers, personal computers, and spreadsheets became more and more necessary.[2] Proponents of utilizing data integration flourished. Bill Inmon, designated the father of data warehousing, referred to this outgrowth as "the corporate wisdom" that needed to be a standard part of the corporate infrastructure.[3]

---

[1]"W. Edwards Deming Quotes." 2019. *Brainyquote*. www.brainyquote.com/quotes/w_edwards_deming_133510

[2]"What Is ETL?" 2019. *Sas.com*. www.sas.com/en_us/insights/data-management/what-is-etl.html

[3]"The Data Warehouse: From the Past to the Present—DATAVERSITY." 2019. *DATAVERSITY*. www.dataversity.net/data-warehouse-past-present/

© Jarrett Goldfedder 2020
J. Goldfedder, *Building a Data Integration Team*, https://doi.org/10.1007/978-1-4842-5653-4_1

Data warehousing was a popular technological breakthrough, and software companies, as they are apt to do in profitable ventures, entered the market with their proprietary solutions. Each market claimed to be better than its competitors, with the result that one department of an organization, perhaps focusing on its own need, would adopt a completely different ETL tool than another department. Thus, contrary to the promises of integration, the promulgation of tools led to an *increase* in data silos, rather than a decrease.

On top of that, the mergers and acquisitions of the dot.com boom forced enterprises to adopt multiple ETL solutions. Each of these had its particular framework, and the entire warehouse solution would need to be either merged into one single system or left as is, thereby relegating the entire architecture into one big mess.

The Current Landscape: Two Distinct Models

As business models have changed to fit the times, so has the ability of organizations to integrate their data, and the approach has taken on a new fashion. Thanks to research and consultancy firms such as Gartner, Inc., popular ETL software have taken on steam; we'll discuss some of my favorite products in Chapter 4. Enterprise systems are slowly switching their focus from on-premise data repositories to cloud-based ones such as AWS Redshift and Microsoft Azure, and developers' abilities to design more modular solutions have eased. From this technological shift, two data integration models have become prevalent:

1. The "data at rest" model whereby the ETL system gathers information across the enterprise and combines records into a consolidated view

2. The "Data Lake" model in which terabytes of data ("Big Data") are combined from multiple different data sources, both structured and unstructured, and analyzed through extremely fast processing engines

These models and the skills required by teams to build them are quite different. For example, the "data at rest" model represents the modern-day corporate data warehouse, usually requiring team members to possess a fair amount of knowledge in database design, architecture design, and ETL development. These systems tend to stay around for the long term, eventually encapsulating a centralized position in the enterprise.

On the other end of the spectrum, the Data Lake models, due to their high volume of streaming data, tend to be more ephemeral, housing data for the short term and generating output on an as-needed basis. For this model, the required skills focus more on Big Data technologies, NoSQL architectures, and data streaming analytics.

These systems can overlap in that some "data at rest" models may contain unstructured data and some "Data Lakes" will have persistent storage. I provide them as examples to denote that we do not create all data repositories the same: different configurations will require vastly different technical skills.

Waterfall Vs. Agile Models

The timeline required to bring the selected data model to fruition also differs. By its very nature, a "data at rest" integration model may require years to perfect versus a Data Lake model based on a stream of Facebook data. For this reason, project teams need to be aware of the potential design issues when scheduling their target delivery dates. This knowledge means that we should avoid a one-size-fits-all strategy. Rather, it is the core team and stakeholders that should define when and how integration requirements and the resulting product should be delivered. In practice, there are two directions we can take:

1. Do the stakeholders expect the analysts to outline the requirements at the beginning of the project with a deliverable prepared at the end?

2. Is the project more of a "define as you go" approach with deliverables established across a series of iterations?

While there can be varying shades of gray between these two spectrums, planning can take the form of either the Waterfall or Agile methodology. Understanding how these two methodologies fit into an integration model is important as they help establish the team-building framework that we discuss throughout this book.

The Waterfall Model

The Waterfall Model, also known as the linear-sequential lifecycle model, was one of the first process models to be introduced into modern organizations. In the waterfall model, a set of phases must be completed before signoff occurs, and the next phase begins.

There is no overlap between phases, with the flow generally a forward-moving, linear process, similar to a moving body of water. As Figure 1-1 illustrates, the Waterfall Model looks exactly like its namesake.

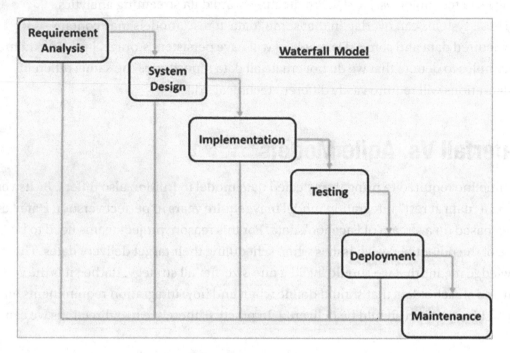

Figure 1-1. *The Waterfall Model*[4]

We see the multiple phases of a waterfall-implemented project, which could be software engineering, construction, or even planning a party—starting with the gathering of requirements, the system design, the implementation, the testing, the deployment, and finally the maintenance. This type of model works well for teams who have a known representation of the tasks ahead and, therefore, can allocate resources based on the task and time required. For example, business analysts can be sourced for a two-week requirement analysis phase, followed by system architects who are brought in for a week to build the design, followed by programmers who code during a four-week implementation phase, and so on.

---

[4]"SDLC—Waterfall Model—Tutorialspoint." 2019. *Tutorialspoint.com.* www.tutorialspoint.com/sdlc/sdlc_waterfall_model.htm

The waterfall model has both its pros and cons.[5] But as one of the first successful project management methodologies, it is still highly regarded in today's business world.

Integration teams brought in to support a waterfall-based project generally join with the rest of the development team—that is, during the implementation phase. This strategy is not always the optimal one, however. Because integration closely aligns with business rules and varying degrees of complexity in terms of source-to-target mappings (STTMs) (which we discuss in the next chapters), a more secure approach is to have some representation of the integration team from the very first meeting, that is, allowing the integration team to provide input and knowledge sharing during the requirement analysis and system design. This representation can consist of face-to-face interaction with a business-facing developer or via proxy from a business analyst with a technical understanding of integration. In any case, I recommend having an integration team member available to discuss technical details from the outset as this involvement will reduce scope creep and architecture modeling issues once project design begins.

The Agile Model

A methodology that has become very popular in software engineering is Agile, which can be traced back to W. Edwards Deming and the application of lean manufacturing principles used by Japanese manufacturing companies to recover from the economic impacts of World War 2.[6]

Agile is more a philosophy than a framework, encouraging a greater level of flexibility, communication, and empowerment over the waterfall model that has rigid start and end dates for each phase. As a differentiator, Agile takes an iterative, collaborative stance with the ability to change course to meet stakeholders' ever-changing needs. It accomplishes this through time-constrained cycles of work known as the *sprint* in which a continuous set of requirements are prioritized and worked until the beginning of the next cycle/sprint (see Figure 1-2).

---

[5]"The Pros and Cons of Waterfall Methodology." 2019. *Lucidchart.com*. www.lucidchart.com/blog/pros-and-cons-of-waterfall-methodology

[6]"The Pros and Cons of Agile Product Development." 2019. *Uservoice Blog*. https://community.uservoice.com/blog/the-pros-and-cons-of-agile-product-development/

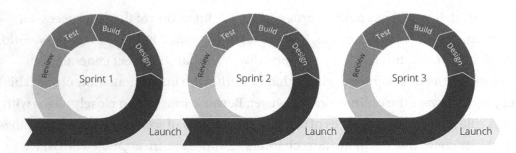

Figure 1-2. *The Sprint Model[7]*

As illustrated, sprints start with prioritizing a set of product deliverables based on requirements (known as "user stories") and have built-in activities for designing, building, testing, reviewing, and, ultimately, product launching. The goal here is not to create a final software product as per the waterfall approach, but rather, to iteratively deliver a series of functions that ultimately contribute to the final product. Although this final product could take weeks or even years to produce, the agile methodology ensures that there is constant forward momentum and (at least in theory) a new update presentable to team members by the end of the sprint.

The Agile model also differs from the waterfall model in that it allows team roles to be flexible and dynamic, requiring the same set of skills to overlap when the group may be "swarming" on the same story at once.[8]

Depending on the individual, teams consisting of specialized integration developers may not be able to join the swarm (and the reverse may be true as the coding team may not possess the prerequisite integration background). While this may appear to go against the grain in terms of the agile philosophy, it is more helpful than you might expect. For one thing, the integration team's tasks are considered a subset of the entire project team, complete with a series of user stories on which they immediately can begin backlog work, collaboration, and sharing. The key here, as with the waterfall model, is to allow the integration members to be a part of the model from the outset, allowing them airtime to voice their concerns, follow up with blockers, and provide management with task updates that may take longer than initially anticipated.

---

[7] "Agile vs. Waterfall: What's the Difference? | Sam Solutions." 2019. *Sam Solutions.* www.sam-solutions.com/blog/waterfall-vs-agile-a-comparison-of-software-development-methodologies/

[8] See "Swarming: A Team-Based Approach to Getting Work Done." 2019. *Medium.* https://medium.com/agile-outside-the-box/swarming-a-team-based-approach-to-getting-work-done-1434243f38b8

Integration Process Vs. Integration Product Ownership

The chosen framework, whether Agile, Waterfall, or a mix in-between, defines the team composition. Equally important are how the team accomplishes their tasks and which individuals should take responsibility for completing them. One of the core concepts for the Agile framework, and to some extent the Waterfall lifecycle model, is product ownership.[9] A *product owner* is a role responsible for managing the product backlog, that is, the items that form the requirements and the shared understanding of the product's problem and solution. The product owner's main responsibility is guiding the development team's direction when multiple competing requirements exist. In the Waterfall model, the equivalent could be the project manager, albeit there are slight differences in the complete set of duties that overlap with a business analyst's role.[10]

From this standpoint, it seems clear that the head of the integration team (the lead integrator that we will discuss in Chapter 3) should own both the product (e.g., the ETL application) and the requirements behind the integration.

But there is another tier of ownership that often remains obscured until the design work: that of *process* ownership, the approach needed to fulfill the mission, vision, tactics, goals, objectives, and measures that will make the integration portion of the project a success (see, for example, `https://www.brcommunity.com/articles.php?id=b668`).

Confusion often arises around this concept because new teams assume that the lead integrator role will own the project backlog items, own the process design, and also support the product ETL software. Consequently, these teams expect that the lead integrator will straddle the line between product owner and developer, two very distinct roles in the Agile model. Care must be taken not to make the role more encompassing than it needs to be. This "double-duty" assignment of product owner/developer tends to fall apart in practice as lead integrators take on the tasks of running the sprint, the project, the solution and managing all development efforts in between. It is often too much for a single person to manage. Thus, I believe it is better to divvy up the non-process-related portions of Agile such as standups and backlog grooming to other team leaders while the lead integrator manages all duties related to running the integration process such as architecture, design, and development.

---

[9]"What Is a Product Owner?" 2019. *Agile Alliance.* `www.agilealliance.org/glossary/product-owner`

[10]"What's the Difference Between a Project Manager and a Product Owner?" 2019. *Merixstudio. com.* `www.merixstudio.com/blog/difference-project-manager-and-product-owner/`

For a full description of the other roles that comprise the integration team, refer to Chapter 3.

Integration Approaches

Three factors determine the skills and responsibilities required for your team. The first is the data model ("at rest" versus "Data Lake"), the second is the lifecycle framework (Agile versus Waterfall), and the third is the overall *technical complexity* of the integration. We've already discussed the first two factors. The last factor, technical complexity, is another way of saying that the more complex the activities behind the integration, the more skills our team members will need. But what type of skills? And how do we define a complex activity? This distinction is where things get tricky, but a good start is unravelling what I mean by "complex activity."

The two most important traits of integration complexity are *frequency* and *schedule*. In this section, we will discuss the following types of integration approaches along with their unique characteristics:

- One-time migration

- Nightly integration

  - Scheduled service

  - Web service

  - Hybrid approach

One-Time Migration

The one-time migration is perhaps the most common and, generally, the first one that comes to my mind when I define "migration." It is the process of taking an existing data source and populating it into a target destination. The source-to-target system traceability is key here. Although the data can sometimes be a one-to-one direct transformation (i.e., the table names, fields, field types, and data are exact copies of one another), more often than not, the process flow requires several transformations performed through programming code or scripting. These transformations can be complex, and business logic can shift from one day to the next, invariably creating some late nights to meet deployment deadlines. But if prepared correctly with the right resources, diagrams, and documentation, a one-time migration can be relatively smooth.

As its name implies, a one-time migration happens *once*, although delta changes—additional loads that occur if the existing system needs to run in parallel with the new system—can also be part of this categorization. If an existing target system requires the deletion of existing data and then to replace it with new data, we often refer to it as "kill and fill."[11]

Nightly Integration

The nightly integration is a supplement to the one-time migration. After the initial data has loaded, separate data feeds must continue to load external system data into the target system. This follow-up is usually the approach for data warehouses, reporting systems, data marts, or any other type of system that stores data used for analysis and decision-making.

Project leads that already have adopted an integration solution but want additional feeds included may request that the team build a new nightly integration feed to tie into the old one. These projects tend to be less complex than one-time migrations in that the target system is already established, loaded with data, and may have previously set standards for modification and code. I advise caution nonetheless, especially if the data from the new source is untested or does not match the existing schema. There is nothing as disheartening as running an initial data load test only to discover that the records are completely different than what the stakeholders expected, requiring more than an overhaul in modifying the existing target system's design. Therefore, as with a one-time migration, research your inbound data, write good documentation, and plan accordingly.

The nightly integrations will usually occur in the early hours of the morning when the business impact is least susceptible but can, of course, occur during the day (in this situation, purists may change the name to be "daily integration"). The execution frequency is generally once per day, but depending on timeliness required for reporting, it can trigger the moment data is input into the source system. These types of systems are called "real time" or, to be technically accurate, "near-real time" since there is a slight lag in delivery from the source to the target.[12]

---

[11]"Glossary." 2019. *Docs.oracle.com*. https://docs.oracle.com/cd/E12440_01/rpm/pdf/150/html/pos_merch_impg/glossary.htm

[12]"The Difference Between Real Time, Near-Real Time, and Batch Processing in Big Data." 2019. *Syncsort Blog*. https://blog.syncsort.com/2015/11/big-data/the-difference-between-real-time-near-real-time-and-batch-processing-in-big-data/

Timing is a critical feature with data loads, and not having the up-to-date information available when you need it is just as important as where it is sourcing. We can separate integration services into three main categories:

- Scheduled service

- Web service

- Hybrid approach

Scheduled Service

Scheduled service is one in which an ETL tool or similar application retrieves the data in the source system, transforms it, and loads it into a target system at a specific time of day. As defined earlier, this trigger can be set at any time of day, for as many iterations as required. The timer itself is usually a component of the querying tool, although administrators can configure external services such as Task Scheduler (Windows), Launchd (Mac), or cron (Unix) to fire custom code designed to perform the same function.

In most systems, scheduled services are relatively easy to configure, and there are numerous online tutorials available to make the most of their flexibility (an excellent example is at *https://automatetheboringstuff.com/schedulers.html*). In just a few minutes, you can set a nightly integration to fire each weeknight at 2:00 a.m. or pull reporting data only on the last day of the month (February leap years included!). As long as the data is ready for retrieval at a prespecified time, the scheduled service should meet most of your execution needs.

Web Service

A web service enables communication among various applications by using open standards such as HTML, XML, REST, and SOAP.[13] For this approach, a preformatted source message is sent "on demand" to a service provider, which could be a front-end ETL tool or web service broker connected to the target (see Figure 1-3).

---

[13]"What Are Web Services?—Tutorialspoint." 2019. *Tutorialspoint.com.* www.tutorialspoint.com/webservices/what_are_web_services.htm

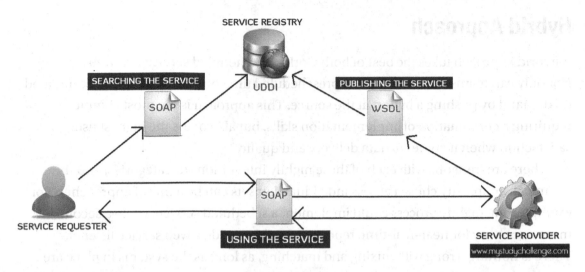

Figure 1-3. *Web Service Architecture[14]*

Responses to the source would include acknowledgment through code along with any errors. This type of custom coding can include many automated notifications sent to various groups along the chain, boosting teams using development operations (DevOps) by alerting the technical staff to issues before your users notice. For example, if the system provides a duplicated record on a unique field and the integration subsequently throws an error, an email notification from the web service can go directly to the business team to make immediate fixes.

Creating this architecture requires more technical skill and testing than standard execution calls. The integration team should have developers who are technically savvy with the implementation of service-oriented architecture[15] as well as business analysts who can deep-dive into the types of errors and alerts that the business users want to receive.

[14]"All You Need to Know About Web Services | My Study Challenge." 2019. *My Study Challenge.* http://mysc.altervista.org/all-you-need-to-know-about-web-services/

[15]For a list of books on the subject, see "Search Results." 2019. *Apress.com.* www.apress.com/us/search?query=SOA

Hybrid Approach

A hybrid approach takes the best of both worlds of scheduled service and web service. Not only can teams execute a job at a prescheduled time but the process can be initiated on demand by pushing a button at the source. This approach is the most complex, requiring a combination of implementation skills, but also offers the highest user satisfaction when it comes to data delivery and quality.

There are tradeoffs with each of these nightly integration subcategories, and the technical complexity chosen across individual datasets can be a mix of approaches. For example, one nightly process could implement a scheduled service, while a second, more necessary for near–real-time reporting, could provide a web service listener. There is nothing wrong with mixing and matching, as long as the systems in place are consistent and well documented. Keep in mind that having too many systems executed constantly or at seemingly random times is just as bad as having none at all. Save yourself the trouble early on and be clear on which one of your implementations can fit under one umbrella.

Designing the project and integration approach is just the first step in putting together a successful integration team. In the next chapter, we elaborate on some of the key terms that will help communicate with the business and technical teams the purpose and need of an integration process.

CHAPTER 2

Key Terms

Technical understanding should be a core competency of any company.

—Edwin Catmull[1]

At this point, we no doubt recognize that starting migration and integration activities are more than just pushing a button and watching data flow from a source to a destination. The process is a reflection of the organization, requiring collaboration across departments, with each representative bringing to the table a unique impression, concern, and perhaps more than one outspoken opinion. Some of these representatives may know very little about what they need in terms of data, while others may profess to know more than they do. Invariably, everyone will need to be on the same page when it comes to building a system integration. The purpose of this chapter is to expose several of the key terms native to the process. By having this common definition from the outset, teams will have productive conversations regarding the integration process components while avoiding much of the confusion that typically accompanies technical solutions.

The Simplicity of Migration

We'll start with a basic diagram. The components of data integration appear to be quite simple.

---

[1] "Edwin Catmull Quotes—Brainyquote." 2019. *Brainyquote.* www.brainyquote.com/authors/edwin-catmull-quotes

© Jarrett Goldfedder 2020
J. Goldfedder, *Building a Data Integration Team,* https://doi.org/10.1007/978-1-4842-5653-4_2

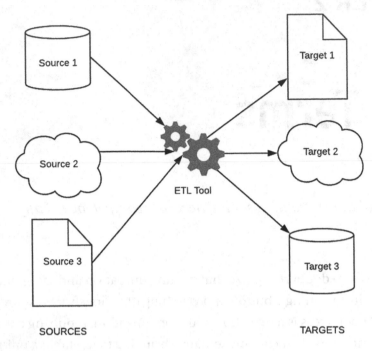

Figure 2-1. *A Simple ETL Diagram*

Figure 2-1 represents a typical migration/integration architecture. We have one or more source systems that deliver a document to a middleware component (ETL tool) that then pushes to one or more target systems. At a high-level this looks fairly easy to implement. With only three components to consider, it is not difficult to understand why the "button-pushing" concept has gained traction.

But dive deeper into the model, lay out the common components of each, and we can see that there is a lot more complexity to this design (see Figure 2-2).

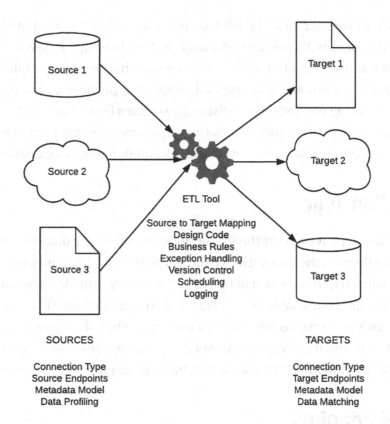

Figure 2-2. *A Not-So-Simple ETL Diagram*

Without previous experience, the challenge that we face is understanding how each of these components will have an impact on our overall solution. Each one needs consideration and a degree of discussion when planning our integration framework.

For the rest of this chapter, we'll be discussing the definition and priority of these components, how they fit with our design, and several examples of how we can best implement them based on the task at hand.

Source System

The source system represents the site housing our inbound data. It represents any repository ranging from comma-separated value (CSV) files to Excel spreadsheets to complex databases and mainframes. In short, any system containing data moved somewhere else is considered a source system.

Naturally, during our initial reviews, there are a lot of questions that arise when discussing our sources. Where are they located? How do we get access to them? What is critical data and where is it stored? It is imperative that the right people—those who work with these systems and understand their designs, purpose and unique process —are present during the first several discovery sessions (see Chapter 4 for a discussion of event sequencing). These individuals should possess the right level of technical knowledge or documentation to provide the information which we discuss here.

Connection Type

The connection type represents the storage location where the data resides. It can be anything that delivers the data such as Excel spreadsheets, databases, text files, and so on. Several subcategories are tied to this as well and may provide necessary details. For example, if the data is available as a text file, is it comma-delimited, tab-delimited, or something else? If the connection type is a database, what plug-ins support it? Knowing these details is particularly important, especially if it requires honing up on esoteric SQL code or finding compatible ETL connectors that support the less popular databases.

Source Endpoints

An endpoint is simply one end of a communication channel.[2] It can be an easy-to-follow URL like *"https://example.com/this-is-an-endpoint/,"* a more complicated WSDL or REST call such as *"http://www.myserver.com/mycustomSite/_vti_bin/excelservice. asmx?WSDL"*, or—if retrieving from the various online cloud or on-premise database systems—available as a JDBC or ODBC connection string such as *"https://www. infocaptor.com/dashboard/jdbc-odbc-drivers-connections-and-strings-url."*

Without the right endpoint, accessing the data can be a challenge. If the stakeholder or business user does not know the endpoint offhand, provided API user manuals may have the answer. Also, in most cases, you will need a username and password that will enable you to log in with the appropriate level of access. By having this information available, you will be able to retrieve (a *GET* method) or input the data (a *POST* method). We'll discuss how this applies to the target endpoint later in the chapter.

---

[2]"Web Services Metadata Exchange (WS-Metadataexchange)." 2019. *W3.org.* www.w3.org/ TR/2011/REC-ws-metadata-exchange-20111213/

Metadata Model

The metadata model is data that describes other data. It summarizes basic information about data, which can make finding and working with other data easier. For example, when you are working with photo images, it is helpful to know the file size or the details behind the type of camera that took the picture.[3] There are at least six object metadata fields that are useful when integrating data:[4]

- Date of Record Creation: Tells you how old a row is

- Who Created Record: Tells you the person (or service account!) that created the record

- Date Record Updated: Tells you how fresh the row is

- Who Updated Record: Tells you whom to talk to get more status about the updated record

- Source of a Record: Tells you which system initially provided this record

- Row Version Number: Tells you how many times a user updated a row

In the data world, the metadata model is also used to reference a data schema in general. For our purposes, this is where the rubber meets the road, especially as you are building the mapping between the source to target fields. Deriving the metadata model for your source and target is mandatory if you want to solidify your integration requirements. Due to its significance, we'll reference the metadata mapping process (called the Source-to-Target Mapping) throughout this book.

[3]"What Is Metadata?—Definition from Whatis.Com." 2019. *Whatis.com*. https://whatis. techtarget.com/definition/metadata

[4]"6 Typical Metadata Fields Stored by Applications—Dataedo Blog." 2019. *Dataedo.com*. https://dataedo.com/blog/typical-metadata-fields-stroed-by-applications

Data Profiling

The effectiveness of your database is only as good as the provided information, and data profiling is the practice of reviewing your source data for content and quality. The main goal is to help us discover the structure, content, and the relationship among our source data.[5] Let's take a closer look at each of these discovery concepts.

Structure Discovery

We expect our data to be formatted consistently. For example, US phone numbers should have ten digits, and US postal codes typically have five. But sometimes the structure may be inconsistent. US phone numbers in our dataset may include office extensions, and US postal codes can include the four-digit extension. Identifying structure exceptions is important when mapping against our comparable target system. For example, if a POSTALCODE field allows for a "19122-2553" format in the source, but then we assume it should be "19122" in the target, our migrated data will be missing structure information that expedites our mail delivery.

Content Discovery

This profiling type involves examining individual data records to find system errors. For example, the postal codes from our previous example might be missing digits due to typos (i.e., four characters instead of five), or the values could be international values stored in the source (e.g., "SW1A 1AA" for the city of London). Content discovery will help us determine what specific rows and fields require correction, allowing us to flag records that we may want to correct in the source before integration.

Relationship Discovery

As systems increase in complexity, so does the interconnectivity among the different components of those systems. Relationship discovery is the process of evaluating how one field connects to another, allowing lookups among different objects. Relationships are critical in many databases, so much so that we commonly refer to databases as relational database management systems (RDBMS).

---

[5]"What Is Data Profiling? Process, Best Practices and Tools." 2019. *Panoply*. https://panoply.io/
analytics-stack-guide/data-profiling-best-practices/

As a simple example, imagine we have a lookup table containing the whole of US postal codes.[6] Now imagine we have a CUSTOMER table with first name, last name, a product, and the address of that user. Rather than repeatedly entering the city, state, and zip code for each user, we could instead supply a key that performs a lookup against the postal code lookup table (see Figure 2-3).

Table: CUSTOMER

CustomerId	First Name	Last Name	Street Address	PostalId
1	John	Smith	1 Main Street	75
2	Sandy	Jones	22 Union Drive	141
3	Terry	Thompson	16 Essex Lane, Apt. 3B	27

Table: POSTALCODE

PostalId	City	State	PostalCode
27	Juneau	Alaska	99802
75	Los Angeles	California	90001
141	Riverton	New Jersey	08077

Figure 2-3. *Relationship Between Customer and PostalCode*

If we examine Figure 2-3, relationship discovery begins to make sense. CUSTOMER. Id #1 (John Smith) contains CUSTOMER.PostalId #75. This value is a direct reference to the POSTALCODE table record for "Los Angeles, California, 90001." Viewed this way, we can see why it is necessary to recognize the relationship between CUSTOMER and POSTALCODE and not just make assumptions that one table is all we need. Without having this understanding of the relationship, you can get very lost in the details, especially if the comparative table in the target system differs widely from the source. To illustrate, let's take our example a step further. For various design reasons, the target CUSTOMER table now contains the complete city, state, and postal code fields (i.e., there is no reference to a PostalId). If you just took the source data and mapped directly to the target, you would have both incomplete as well as inaccessible data. (see Figure 2-4)

Source Table: CUSTOMER

CustomerId	First Name	Last Name	Street Address	PostalId
1	John	Smith	1 Main Street	75
2	Sandy	Jones	22 Union Drive	141
3	Terry	Thompson	16 Essex Lane, Apt. 3B	27

Transform →

Target Table: CUSTOMER

CustomerId	First Name	Last Name	Street Address	City	State	PostalCode
1	John	Smith	1 Main Street	?	?	?
2	Sandy	Jones	22 Union Drive	?	?	?
3	Terry	Thompson	16 Essex Lane, Apt. 3B	?	?	?

Figure 2-4. *Customer Mapping Without PostalCode Relationship Discovery*

---

[6]For starters, see "US Zip Codes Database | Simplemaps.Com." 2019. *Simplemaps.com.* `https://simplemaps.com/data/us-zips`

Figure 2-4 illustrates that the target City, State, and PostalCode values are impossible to populate when the POSTALCODE table is missing from the equation. The moral of this illustration is to ensure that you identify and document *all* tables that make up the entire data view and not just go with the assumed one-to-one match approach.

ETL Tool

The extraction, transformation, and loading (ETL) portion of our model is made up of both the middleware platform (i.e., an on-premise or cloud-based server) and the software that compiles code designed for integrating the data from the source to the target. Any system that can pull or receive (extract) data from the source system, perform modifications through a sequence of processing steps (transformation), and then push (load) this data into a target designation qualifies as an ETL tool. This part of the architecture is where most of the lift and hardwiring for the integration team will occur, so picking the right ETL platform and software is crucial.

We cover ETL software and design in later chapters. For now, we'll introduce the standard technical components that comprise the ETL model.

Source-to-Target Mapping

For the data integration team, the source-to-target mapping (STTM) is a set of instructions that determine how to convert the data from the source system into the proper structure and content required by the target system.[7] At its most basic, the STTM includes only the relevant source metadata, transformation rules, and target metadata. There are many more details that you can provide, and the more complex solutions will probably require them. We'll discuss more about these optional fields in Chapter 4.

Design Code

Nothing confusing here. The design code is merely the code that extracts, transforms, and loads the data from the source to the target. But as the brains behind the whole integration process, the design code configuration rests entirely on the chosen ETL

---

[7]"What Is Source-to-Target Mapping? | Knowledge Center | Lore IO." 2019. *Getlore.io*. www.getlore.io/knowledgecenter/source-to-target-mapping

software. Some user interfaces are graphic drop-and-drag, while others require programming against proprietary libraries that work only with Java, JavaScript, .NET, or any of the other myriad programming languages currently available. As with everything else we have discussed, careful consideration is essential in finding the right code for the right job and then ensuring that team members have the appropriate coding skills.

Business Rules

These are the lists of statements that supply criteria and conditions for transforming your data from the source to the target. Business Rules differ from business requirements in that *business requirements* are the things with which you need to comply to enable rules.[8] Although Business Rules should be fixed and consistent, more often than not, they can lead to some heated exchanges among business owners who may disagree on what rule should be applied to which data. Fortunately, these discussions are organized mostly around the target system since the populated source system, by definition, already contains data that has an originating business rule. Still, don't be misled by thinking that the business rules in the provided source system will transfer directly to the target system as is. In many cases, updated business decisions will drive new business rules, which, in turn, could require transforming the outbound data into something quite different from its inbound format.

Exception Handling

Data migration and integration processes can fail for two main reasons—either technical due to a network or database connectivity issue or business related due to data failing an expected business rule. Under these circumstances, the data team and business owners need to be made aware of the failure. But how should this happen? Through online log notifications? Through email? Through a third-party application? The specification of alerts and similar errors is known as exception handling and should be designed based on the built-in software configurations, the design code, or both.[9]

---

[8]For an excellent analogy, see Lam, Gladys. 2019. "Business Rules vs. Business Requirements: Commentary—Business Rules Community/Business Rules Journal." *Business Rules Community—BRC*. www.brcommunity.com/articles.php?id=b290

[9]Mitchell, Tim. 2019. "ETL Error Handling." *Tim Mitchell web site*. www.timmitchell.net/post/2016/12/28/etl-error-handling/

Version Control

Data loading can involve much trial-and-error testing with design code changes happening frequently. What was once a retrieval of a few fields from the source can quickly cascade into multiple tables, with each one bearing a dependency on the one before it. Every time you modify a file function, you unintentionally risk breaking a different part of your code. Over time, it becomes difficult to track all your changes. The right thing to do would be to take an occasional pause and back up the existing code base, but doing so can bloat your computer with incremental change files that you may never need to open. One solution to keeping your file safe and recoverable is through version control, a system that records changes to a file or set of files over time so that you can recall specific versions later.[10]

Version control systems (VCSs) have been in use for decades, mostly for software applications that have periodic minor releases and bug fixes. But the use has become more common with any component that requires scripting, ETL software included. I can personally attest that it's worth the effort. On one occasion, I accidentally mistyped a Unix command to remove what I thought was an insignificant file and then ended up removing the entire directory consisting of 25 extremely important files. Fortunately, I was able to roll back my deletion through the magic of VCS reversion.[11] My recommendation for you is to adopt the same strategy for your code design backups.

Scheduling

If the ETL process is repeatable, that is, running at a particular time of day on a specified interval, then the process can be set to auto-execute. The way to set this execution is through a scheduled service which might be built-in to the ETL tool or configured through a server scheduling application. For more details on job scheduling as part of a nightly integration approach, refer to Chapter 1, Scheduled Services.

---

[10]"Git—About Version Control." 2019. *Git-scm.com*. https://git-scm.com/book/en/v2/Getting-Started-About-Version-Control

[11]"How to Undo the Last Commit." 2019. *Medium*. https://code.likeagirl.io/how-to-undo-the-last-commit-393e7db2840b

Logging

Integration jobs can run in parallel and execute at any time of the day. With so much traffic passing through the ETL tool, creating a moment-by-moment status report for each record success or failure might be overkill. We want to avoid loading our server with too much information. At the same time, however, we still might want to store this information *just in case,* especially if we work with data that might have legal or financial ramifications to the organization. As a simple example, imagine we have designed and deployed an ETL process for a magazine publication. This process performs a nightly integration against customer subscriptions by copying records from a source accounting system to a target mailing list. Everything that we've built up to now appears to be running smoothly.

But wait, not so fast. Two weeks after deployment, our customer service department receives a complaint from an irate customer who claims that she has been receiving a magazine to which she never subscribed. "Impossible," we say, knowing that our ETL system has worked fine up to now. But a query into our subscription database reveals that this customer truly was assigned the wrong magazine. How could that have happened? And when?

The most efficient way to investigate would be by going through log files to trace the moment when the record and mismatched subscription entered the ETL system. Most ETL tools can provide this logging functionality, the individual inbound and outbound recordsets, and the time, date, and name of the job process that executed. Due to their large file size over time, the system should be configured to keep log files just long enough to investigate any issues that may arise—perhaps three weeks to a month. Keeping them longer may cause your system to falter as processing space decreases. Without these logs on hand, however, it could take days or even weeks to uncover the root cause, all the while having to deal with customers and business owners who become increasingly annoyed with what they can only surmise is *your* faulty integration logic, as opposed to a completely unrelated event.

Target

The target system receives the integration data and often represents the key deliverable of an integration project. Most of the business rules that require adjusting or tweaking are for the benefit of the target system, and these particular stakeholders are the ones that need to be comfortable with the integration team's solutions. The connection type and metadata model components in the target are the same as discussed earlier with the source, with the same approximate fundamentals. The target endpoints and data matching concepts do differ, however, and we'll cover them here.

Target Endpoint

The target endpoint is the receiving channel of the data stream that originated in the source, extracted to the ETL, and then is loaded to fit existing business rules. The main difference between the target and source endpoint is from the perspective of the ETL connector. The connector retrieves from the source using a GET method and pushes it to the target using a POST method.[12] That is about as much as I can say on web services without diving deeper into the topic, so for now, just be aware of the difference between GET and POST. If you want to know more, I recommend reading Sanjay Patni's book, *Pro RESTful APIs* (Apress, 2017).[13]

Data Matching

The target system contains records from multiple datasets. If you think about it, having a common identifier for all these systems would be rare. Even a common table such as CONTACT might use a national identity value such as Social Security Number as the unique identifier from one source and then shift to a passport number as the unique identifier from a second source. The role of data matching is to find records that refer to the same entity, often by analyzing across fields that provide partial identification, such as a full name or date of birth.[14] Finding these common identifiers can be challenging when importing across multiple source systems. As an aid, software companies have created specialized scripts, algorithms, and software to merge and minimize duplicate records. From this point onward, the data matching crosses into a technical arena known as Master Data Management (MDM), so named because a single record (the "master")

[12]"HTTP Methods—REST API Verbs—REST API Tutorial." 2019. *Restfulapi.net*. https:// restfulapi.net/http-methods/

[13]Patni, Sanjay. 2019. "*Pro Restful APIs: Design, Build and Integrate with REST, JSON, XML and JAX-RS* | Sanjay Patni | Apress." *Apress.com*. www.apress.com/us/book/9781484226643

[14]"What Is Data Matching?" 2019. *Medium*. https://medium.com/neuronio/ what-is-data-matching-9478c80da888

can theoretically trace back to the source system identifiers, centralizing enterprise databases into a single hub.[15] Designing an MDM requires a different set of skills from integration and won't be covered in our topics. Do keep in mind, however, that a data matching approach in the target system is a step closer to achieving MDM, the ultimate goal in reconciling data across an enterprise.

We've covered many of the key terms and concepts in this chapter, starting with the simple diagram of an integration architecture. Underneath the surface of the proverbial data iceberg, there's more to take in. Now that we understand the mechanics of the source, ETL, and the target systems, we can now begin to highlight the required skills. Specifically, what roles and responsibilities do we need in our integration team? The next chapter will dive into detail.

---

[15]"What Is Master Data Management (MDM) and Why Is It Important?" 2019. *Searchdatamanagement.* https://searchdatamanagement.techtarget.com/definition/ master-data-management

CHAPTER 3

Team Qualifications

But what I do have are a very particular set of skills, skills I have acquired over a very long career.

—Liam Neeson, Taken (2008)[1]

In the previous chapters, we've discussed the basics of integration, approaches, and some of the key terms. With this understanding, we can now start talking about the roles and responsibilities required to make an integration project successful.

Many project leaders believe that one person can be responsible for an entire integration effort, including requirements, design, and the inevitable deployment. In some situations, this is true. But in many others, additional support is needed. Unfortunately, as with all projects that have multiple layers of complexity, the types of skills and the number of resources required to support are unknown long after kickoff begins.

Throughout this chapter, we will talk about the subtle and not-so-subtle best practices that make up the integration team:

- Team personality

- Types of teams

- Team sizes

- Waterfall versus Agile team expectations

- Integration team roles

- Recruiting your team

---

[1] "Liam Neeson Taken Quotes Are Everything You Need Ever." 2019. *Mandatory.* www.mandatory.com/culture/1308735-liam-neeson-taken-quotes

© Jarrett Goldfedder 2020
J. Goldfedder, *Building a Data Integration Team*, https://doi.org/10.1007/978-1-4842-5653-4_3

After reading this chapter, you will have a clearer picture of how to build the integration team, when to shift the "single person does it all" mind-set, and, perhaps most importantly, how you can best enhance the staff and skills that will make your projects successful.

Team Personality

Personality matters. For your teams, there will always be those who prefer to collaborate with others compared to those who would instead do it alone, at least for most of the daily tasks. We tend to define these personalities as extroversion versus introversion,[2] but because of its collaborative nature, integration activities will require team members to have strengths in both areas. Your integration architect and ETL developers must work closely with stakeholders across teams to gather requirements and then clarify them as needed (sometimes at the last minute!). However, these same people must also have a penchant for the introversion needed for marathon research and design, often deep-diving into technical code that requires attention to detail.

With this understanding in mind, having a single-person mind-set—an individual who can accomplish the entire integration process—is possible, but daunting to say the least. And for the sake of sanity, if such a person is available, the amount of work assigned to them is probably best left for the short term; a permanent role is both demoralizing and can lead to burnout.

I am not suggesting that those who identify themselves more as extroverts will do better or worse in a particular integration role than those who identify themselves as introverts. But for the sake of team harmony, people who can both focus on the technical side of things and be appropriately outgoing result in more collaboration and communication, a necessity for these types of projects. In any case, people tend to be stronger in either one area or the other,[3] and it is essential to note whether people would much rather work on a team, alone, or both and then assign them the integration activities that best fit that role.[4]

---

[2]2019. *Myersbriggs.org*. www.myersbriggs.org/my-mbti-personality-type/mbti-basics/extraversion-or-introversion.htm?bhcp=1

[3]For my favorite analyses, see "Free Personality Test, Type Descriptions, Relationship and Career Advice | 16Personalities." 2019. *16personalities.com*. www.16personalities.com/

[4]Parris, Jennifer. 2019. "Teamwork vs. Individual Work: Would You Rather Work on a Team or Alone?" *Flexjobs Job Search Tips and Blog*. www.flexjobs.com/blog/post/how-to-answer-would-you-rather-work-on-a-team-or-alone/

Types of Teams

In all honesty, an integration project can be a one-size-fits-all approach: gather a group of technical and functional team members who have a common goal or interest, give them the space to resolve integration requirements, build the code specific to those requirements, and then perform the duties of testing. Iteration, deployment, and monitoring. Figure 3-1 shows the process flow at a high level.

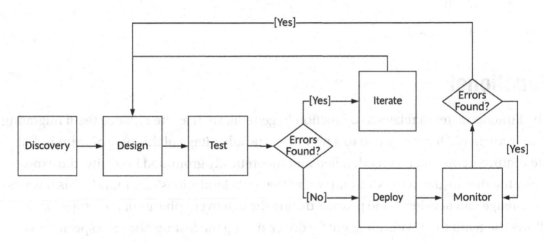

Figure 3-1. *Integration Flowchart*

Basic Team Flow

We will discuss the elements of the integration flow in greater detail in Chapter 4, but for now, understand that the type of team we establish is essential because it emphasizes how fast and how effectively the flow among these activities will be. For example, if the integration involves moving data from a legacy finance application into a cloud-based one, some activities flow faster if the team consists of just the Finance team versus one purely of IT. Or perhaps the representatives chosen are a blend of departmental functions such as HR, Accounting, Customer Relationship Management, and so on.

The type of team approach you choose will depend on what works best with the expected deliverables, and adapting throughout the project may be necessary until teams feel they have achieved the right momentum. There are four types of teams[5] we will consider:

- Functional

- Cross-Functional

- Virtual

- Self-directed

Functional

The Functional team relates to a function in general, such as the Finance team migrating data from an old legacy system to a new one. The advantage of this type of team is that the requirements will be very detailed and theoretically grounded in reality: the experts know the day-to-day processes and where the "data landmines" are found. This business knowledge can accelerate the process during the discovery phases of the project and allows the team to provide excellent feedback during the testing phases, especially as these data landmines systematically are defused.[6]

The biggest negative of the Functional team is the same as the benefit in that too many cooks can spoil the soup. The more experts on a project, the more perspectives you invite with the unfortunate result of frequent debate, group polarization,[7] and hard-to-avoid "paralysis by analysis."[8] One of the better methods for diluting this effect is to keep the number of experts in the room during the integration phases to a minimum, that is, generally no more than two. There will be some initial questions or unknowns,

---

[5]"Learn Quality Management, ISO 9001, Six Sigma, and Data Analysis." 2019. *Quality Gurus*. www.qualitygurus.com/4-types-of-teams/

[6]"Bad Data That Changed the Course of History." 2019. *Datafloq.com*. https://datafloq.com/read/bad-data-that-changed-the-course-of-history/3032

[7]Psychology, Social. 2019. "Group Polarization (SOCIAL PSYCHOLOGY)—Iresearchnet." *Psychology.iresearchnet.com*. https://psychology.iresearchnet.com/social-psychology/group/group-polarization/

[8]"9 Tips to Avoid Paralysis by Analysis." 2019. *Behavioral Science in the 21st Century*. https://bsci21.org/9-tips-to-avoid-paralysis-by-analysis/

and these can be shared with the broader team once the standard, less debatable issues are confirmed. Of course, you should document and share all meeting notes to avoid surprises with the familiar complaint, "Why wasn't I included in this decision?"[9]

Because of their technical nature, integrations will, at some point, require a development team to step in. Functional teams may or may not have knowledgeable staff who can conduct these phases. For that reason, I would recommend that the functional team handling all aspects of the discovery and testing phases should begin handing off work to the developers with close supervision. This level of review should ensure that the developers interpret the requirements with clear understanding.

Cross-Functional

Integration projects that span across systems with multiple purposes will want to utilize the Cross-Functional team. As an example, imagine that instead of integrating a legacy finance app in a new system, we are now moving an entire accounting system from ground to cloud. This new application would feature paycheck information, employee data, and purchase orders. In other words, this scope crosses multiple functionalities.

As with a single Functional team, the Cross-Functional team will need to bring in the experts from the specific departments. Unlike the Functional team, however, the Cross-Functional team members must *work with each other* since the new system overlaps. Human Resources and Employee Relations might both require data stored within the same table, and these departments will need to agree on the format of this data. As a simple example, if State is a shared field in an ADDRESS table and Human Resources uses an abbreviation (AK, AL, AZ), while Employee Relations uses the full spelling (Alaska, Alabama, Arizona), then the result, known colloquially as the "Golden Record" or "Single Point of Truth" (SPOT),[10] must be honored (see Figure 3-2).

---

[9]"How to Encourage Employee Involvement in Decision Making." 2019. *Forbes.com*. www.forbes.com/sites/mikekappel/2018/04/04/how-to-encourage-employee-involvement-in-decision-making/#9b981d16561c

[10]Golombek, Anne. 2019. "The Holy Grail of Data Intelligence: The Single Point of Truth." *Blog.minubo.com*. https://blog.minubo.com/en/ecommerce-insights/data-intelligence-single-point-of-truth/

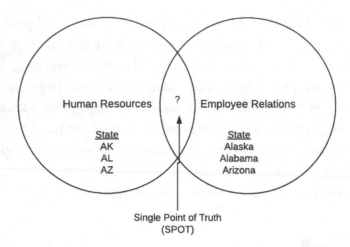

Single Point of Truth
(SPOT)

Figure 3-2. *Cross-Functional Agreement*

Cross-Functional teams have a similar advantage to the Functional team in that the business members know their subject matter and can be very helpful in defining requirements and performing tests. But, as noted earlier, data formats open to disagreement and overlap may require mediation. At this point, teams should demonstrate excellent communication, tradeoffs, and compromises. I have personally seen meetings go off the tracks due to unanticipated displays of passion from a disagreeable team member.

Once the cross-functional team has worked together for a while, an interesting phenomenon occurs. Known as the performing stage of team formation,[11] team members establish a level of mutual respect and trust, and members begin to work closely with one another. This stage is where the real advantage of a cross-functional team comes into play. Similar to living in a different culture, teams from separate departments begin to understand and accept the work and processes performed by their coworkers. That makes sense since, after all, they have been eating, breathing, and reading these viewpoints from the beginning of the project. This acceptance, in turn, leads to an improved understanding of different facets of the organization. For me, this type of knowledge and approval can only happen when teams from different units must work together toward a common goal. Although it occurs only once in a while, the bonding within the cross-functional integration team can be the most satisfying in

---

[11]"Forming, Storming, Norming, and Performing: Understanding the Stages of Team Formation." 2019. *Mindtools.com.* www.mindtools.com/pages/article/newLDR_86.htm

terms of leaving one's comfort zone to learn something new as well as establish long-term friendships with people whose interests and skills might be vastly different than your own.

Virtual Team

If working in a cross-functional team is like blending different cultures, the virtual integration team might be the real deal. Although not always, this type of team consists of people from different cultures and different languages, working together to achieve the same goal. As virtual teams have become more common in the last decade, the team might also be people who, for one reason or another, work remotely from a home office, coffee shop, or other network-accessible location. The point is that the teams are not physically in the same space and must use technology for communication.

The advantage of the virtual team comes in threes: productivity, teamwork, and presence.[12] In the tech world, the 9–5 existence has become obsolete,[13] and lack of a commute means less time traveling and more time online. As the demand for offshore engineers develops and network technology improves, the virtual team is slowly becoming the framework of the future.

I love the rainy-day Google Hangouts as much as the next person, but I am sad to say that the advantages of virtual communication do not seem to work in the early phases of integration. Let me stress that I base this finding on my personal experience (so no angry letters, virtual or otherwise, please). As we've discussed, gathering requirements involves direct collaboration and communication, which means face-to-face conversations, body language readings, voiced guidance, and in-person clarifications. I have found that what usually would take 5 minutes to cover in a face-to-face meeting could take hours to explain through a series of emails or video conversations. This delay in having questions answered often leads to a growing backlog and forced priorities as one misunderstood table dependency can cascade into gaps in requirements.

Enough about the bad news. The good news is that, from a development standpoint, integration projects and virtual teams work very well with one another. With cloud-based security and network connectivity through remote logins and VPNs, the benefits

---

[12]"Why Remote Workers Are Outperforming Office Workers." 2019. *Inc.com.* www.inc.com/brian-de-haaff/3-ways-remote-workers-outperform-office-workers.html

[13]Goffeney, Katherine. 2019. "The 9-to-5 Workday Isn't Just Hated—It's Obsolete." *Quartz at Work.* https://qz.com/work/1189605/the-9-to-5-workday-isnt-just-hated-its-obsolete/

of virtual work are readily transparent. As an example, during a six-hour flight to the West Coast, I completed five fixes and held two conference calls (sorry, passengers in Row 23, I'll be quieter next time). Of course, when you hit a speed bump in terms of a requirements question, your productivity can screech to a halt.

So how do you deal with the constant speedup and then drag to productivity? The answer is to allow your team to have both virtual and onsite days (if you can, that is). Pick one or two days of the week where very little happens in the way of requirements sessions and make that your team's "virtual work" day. The other days of the week will be onsite and will allow you to focus exclusively on those priorities that will impact your productivity. Of course, depending on the amount of backlog and complexity of work, you may have to be onsite for some weeks during kickoff and discovery or virtual for other weeks during development. The choice is up to you and your organization's policy. Just remember some things are better in person and might be worth the extra effort if your team finds itself falling deeper into backlog despair.

Self-Directed Team

Self-directed teams consist of people who see a problem and then come together on their own to resolve that problem. With these types of teams, there's no clear hierarchy in the beginning, but roles and responsibilities are slowly divvied up based on the work individuals want to complete. As an example, individuals in our Finance team have migrated their cloud-based system. Now they want to receive reports from a reporting database that does not yet exist. Although not a mandate from management, the team decides to build the database and code on the side.

The impacts for the self-directed team to NOT complete the project are often low since the success and failure of the workstream have no direct effect on the organization. It is just a "nice-to-have" that allows the same advantages as the other three types of teams while leading to some inventions that have considerable upside. Art Fry invented the Post-it through self-directed experimentation, and it changed the path of 3M forever.[14] A self-directed integration team could theoretically turn an idea into a killer app if the timing and skills fall into alignment.

---

[14]"How 3M Gave Everyone Days Off and Created an Innovation Dynamo." 2019. *Fast Company*. www.fastcompany.com/1663137/how-3m-gave-everyone-days-off-and-created-an-innovation-dynamo

Team Sizes

What is the right size for an integration team? There are no hard and fast rules, although software development literature identifies significant correlations between team size and productivity.[15] As a rule of thumb, software development productivity is higher for smaller teams from three to five staff, with similar values up to seven. After around nine or more people, effort and cost exponentially are shown to rise. The scrum framework agrees with this assessment, stating that between three and nine people are the optimum size and team size should not go beyond that.[16] By comparison, the waterfall model disagrees, and team sizes can be quite large, often more than 15 people.[17]

Integration differs from software development in that the work tends to be more consistent and repeatable (at least in terms of ETL design principles; see Chapter 4). We've talked about the single-person approach to following the integration process flow of discovery through monitoring, and while such work is technically possible for the short term, it can be overwhelming once the testing issues and bug fixes start to land in the queue. I've been on integration teams with as little as two people (a project manager and an integration architect), and I find that this works relatively well for small projects that require fast turnaround. If the timeline can extend, a three-person team will introduce a business analyst to the mix (i.e., a project manager, an integration architect, and a business analyst), while a four-person team is optimal for training junior ETL developers against simple, one-stop designs (i.e., a project manager, an integration architect, a business analyst, and an ETL developer). An integration team assigned more than four people means that the organization is taking the data efforts seriously. In this case, recruiting and training technically minded individuals with front-facing skills becomes a priority.

---

[15]D. Rodríguez, M. A. Sicilia, E. García, and R. Harrison. 2012. "Empirical Findings on Team Size and Productivity in Software Development." *Journal of Systems and Software* 85 (3): 562–570. doi:10.1016/j.jss.2011.09.009.

[16]"The 3 Bears of Agile Team Size—Rgalen Consulting." 2019. *Rgalen Consulting.* http://rgalen.com/agile-training-news/2015/8/22/the-3-bears-of-agile-team-size

[17]"Roles in Waterfall Methodology." 2019. *Hygger.* https://hygger.io/blog/team-roles-in-waterfall-methodology/

Waterfall Vs. Agile Team Expectations

We've discussed team sizes and how they fit with the Waterfall versus Agile methodology. But before we can go further and discuss the roles themselves, we must also mention the level of participation expected from team members. As with team size, we cannot assume that responsibilities will be the same. Waterfall and agile are comparatively different, and this difference will influence your hiring and training approaches.[18] Let's dive a bit deeper.

Waterfall

As we discussed in an earlier chapter, Waterfall is one of the first modern lifecycle models with a strict structure from beginning to end. This same fixation on structure applies to team members, all of whom are responsible for completing (or "owning") a specific stage of work. For example, business analysts own and hand off just the business requirements, software developers own and hand off the code and other pertinent deliverables, and the integration participants own and handle anything related to that aspect. As projects grow, so do the levels of responsibility. This task ownership is partly the reason why team sizes for Waterfall-based projects can rise well into the double digits.

Agile

In contrast to Waterfall projects, agile teams are usually small with interchangeable team members. Think of the team more as a swarm in which a problem arises and each member can then step in to resolve. Thus, rather than focusing on owning a specific stage of work, the team is self-managing and will solve project issues through communication and agreement rather than role specification.

Best Approaches

Figure 3-3 represents the team composition for the cross-functional (Agile) versus specialized (Waterfall) roles. Each letter of the illustration represents a different team member, and each color represents a different skill.

---

[18]"Agile and Waterfall Teams." 2019. *Hygger.* https://hygger.io/blog/agile-and-waterfall-teams/

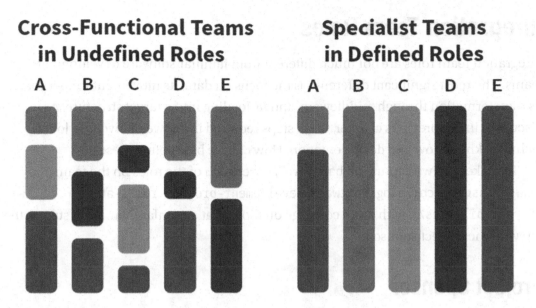

Figure 3-3. *Cross-Functional Teams Vs. Specialist Teams[19]*

Both teams have five team members, but the Agile one on the left requires the members to possess a variety of skills. If sponsoring a waterfall project as shown on the right, you will want your integration team members to be focused on one specialization at any given time, what is called a *defined role*. Hiring and training for the Agile integration team should, therefore, focus on knowledge breadth, while a defined role for the Waterfall integration team should focus on knowledge depth.

The T-Shaped Person

Ideally, the type of employee you would want over the long term would be one known as a "T-shaped" person with the base knowledge and skills needed for cross-functional work and in-depth knowledge in one or two additional specialties. Finding people with these characteristics may appear complicated at the outset, but there are some tips and tricks that can improve the T-shaped set of knowledge and skills. An excellent article to start with is at *https://collegeinfogeek.com/become-t-shaped-person/*.[20]

---

[19]"1.1.4 Waterfall and Agile | Project Resources." 2019. *Projectresources.cdt.ca.gov*. https:// projectresources.cdt.ca.gov/agile/waterfall-and-agile/

[20]Patterson, Ransom. 2019. "The T-Shaped Person: Building Deep Expertise and a Wide Knowledge Base." *College Info Geek*. https://collegeinfogeek.com/become-t-shaped-person/

Integration Team Roles

Integration team roles are not much different from familiar software development teams. The most significant difference is the focus on data, its movement from a source, its transformation through middleware, and its loading into a target structure. As we discussed in the previous chapter, these steps required in-between involve a lot of technical know-how and documentation. How can we best define these?

To make sure we capture all bases, we'll cover each of the roles on the team (`www.atlascode.com/blog/software-development-project-roles-and-responsibilities/`), with more coverage on those that are unfamiliar. We'll start at the top with the project sponsor.

Project Sponsor

The project sponsor is the person (or group) who provides direction, the resource, and—to put it bluntly—the funding for the project. Ultimately, the project sponsor has the most financial investment to ensure the project's success.

Stakeholders

The stakeholders represent the person or groups who have interest or concern in the project from the organization's perspective. This role is greatly affected by the organization's actions, objectives, and policies and has a vested interest in the success or failure of the project at hand. Stakeholders are not just employees, but can also consist of creditors, directors, owners, suppliers, and unions.[21]

Subject Matter Expert (SME)

These are the people who know the fundamental details of a business, technical, or organizational perspective. During a data integration project, the subject matter experts will be able to provide the requirements and also talk about the day-to-day operations of their respective departments.

---

[21]"Definition: Stakeholder." 2019. *Businessdictionary.com*. `www.businessdictionary.com/definition/stakeholder.html`

I should mention that due to their responsibilities in keeping departments running smoothly, SMEs spend a lot of time going from one meeting to another, or putting out a symbolic fire. Receiving a 1:1 audience with a subject matter expert is not a trivial matter, and the earlier in the process you can meet, the better. Have good questions because often, the SME is the only one who can answer them accurately.

Product Owner

The product owner role is highlighted more in an Agile project than Waterfall, although modern software ownership blurs the line, and I have seen this role described in both. This person determines what features will be in the product release for a specific application, documents user stories, and is the main point of contact for all decisions related to the project.

Project Manager (PM)

If a Waterfall project were an orchestra, the project manager would be its conductor. This person knows the ins and outs of the software project, manages the budget and the schedule, oversees the software testing, delivers all documentation, and gets formal acceptance by the customer.

In an integration project, the project manager continues to maintain that role, leaning heavily on the technical lead as needed, but continuing to serve as the interface between the development team and customer.

Technical Lead

In a software development project, this person translates the business requirements into a technical solution and assigns activities to the software developers. In the integration portion of a project, the data integration architect may replace the role of the technical lead.

Data Integration Architect

The data integration architect is part of the IT team and, as the title suggests, works on data integration solutions. Data integration architects specialize in their field, managing all aspects of a data architecture that involve the movement of data from one point to another. These job roles also tend to be customer-facing and include working closely with teams of ETL developers in the same capacity as the technical lead. The main difference, of course, focuses on the integration side of the house, which requires different functional and technical skills than software development.

Software Developers

The software developers are responsible for using the technical requirements from the technical lead to create cost and timeline estimates, build deliverables, and communicate the status of the project to the technical lead and project manager. In an integration project, ETL developers replace the role of software developers, although the duties are relatively the same.

Software Testers

Software testers ensure that the software solution meets the business requirements and is free of bugs, errors, and defects. As with software developers, we could rename this role to *ETL tester*, but that is a bit more awkward. We often stick with the more generic-sounding title of *tester* to represent both.

User Acceptance Testers

These people are the representatives from the company who perform the final checks to ensure that the software works for the business across several real-world scenarios. In the integration team, the user acceptance testers should be those who handle the day-to-day data activities and would thus have the most precise conception on whether the integration performs as expected.

Business Analyst

The business analyst is responsible for bridging the gap between IT and the business. They do this through data analytics, requirements gathering, process assessment, and delivering data-driven recommendations and reports to senior executives and stakeholders. Business analysts create initiatives and strategies that will improve importing and optimize costs and often have finance teams and IT as their customers. Business analysts also focus on data-driven tasks such as budgeting and forecasting, planning and monitoring, pricing, reporting, and defining business requirements.

For an integration project, the business analyst works as the liaison between the functional and technical sides, ensuring that business requirements are accurate and interpreted correctly by the ETL developers. There is a continuous back-and-forth aspect to this role as the business analyst must confirm that what the developer heard is what the stakeholders meant.

Release Manager

The release manager is a relatively new role, which has achieved wide recognition in the world of development operations (DevOps) and is worth discussing from an integration standpoint.[22] This person owns the release management lifecycle, consisting of the scheduling, coordinating, and management of releases for multiple applications. The releases can be inclusive of application updates, operating system patches, security improvements, hardware upgrades, projects, programs, and so on.

The release manager plays a vital role in testing and deploying integrations within the ETL application and must work collaboratively with all participants, including the ETL developers and testers, as they set up their build, test, and production environments.

The position requires more of a T-shaped skillset than other ones discussed. As automation across industries continues to advance, the role of the integration release manager may shift to a universal tester; but, for the time being, this person serves as the gatekeeper between the different environments and has their hands full with ensuring systems continually process the data.

Recruiting Your Team

Now that we've talked about the various roles within the teams, it's time to identify and recruit those individuals who will be working with you. Your first step, of course, is to determine what type of role you need and then to create the job description.

---

[22]"Release Manager: The Definitive Job Description." 2019. *Plutora*. www.plutora.com/blog/release-manager-job

Determining the Roles

There are two ways to evaluate the context of your integration project:

- A supplemental add-on in which the integration is the secondary part of a much larger project

- A primary project which is a large-scale, perhaps enterprise-style deployment

Many of the initial projects you work on will be of the first type, but if the organization is moving toward repository or data warehouse initiatives, the second type will crop up. In any case, when you decide the roles you need to hire, you must consider the big picture. Naturally, if running the supplemental integration, you will want to start with the standard software development team and add at a minimum the roles for integration architect, ETL developer, and business analyst. Because these types of projects tend to be short term, you will also need to consider if you would want to hire an independent contractor or stick with a permanent full-time employee who could perform double-duty work once the project had ended or lapses.

Independent contractors can also be a part of the longer, large-scale projects, but the skills and requirements you need fit more into the T-shaped qualifications we discussed earlier, which would necessitate hiring more seasoned professionals, perhaps adding training as the practice builds out.

For more on the pros and cons of contract versus full-time staffing, refer to *https:// blog.toggl.com/contract-vs-full-time/*.[23]

The Job Description

Knowing whether you want short- or long-term employment is the key to writing a good job description. You want to provide enough details for candidates to evaluate their qualifications while managing to keep the summary concise. As a rule of thumb, Indeed. com recommends keeping the description between 700 and 2,000 characters long.[24]

---

[23]Neely, Joe. 2019. "Contract vs. Full-Time Employees: How to Make the Right Decision—Toggl Blog." *Toggl Blog*. https://blog.toggl.com/contract-vs-full-time/

[24]"How to Write a Job Description | Indeed.Com." 2019. *Indeed.com*. www.indeed.com/hire/ how-to-write-a-job-description

In terms of staffing your integration project, you will want to include sampler boilerplate text for the job duties. I recommend also adding the following topics:

- Job Experience: The more complicated the integration requirements, the more years of integration-specific experience that you will want your candidate to have.

- Education: Many integration roles want Computer Science or Mathematics as a background, but this does not necessarily need to be the case. I've seen many good Business majors make excellent integration leads as the ability to communicate with stakeholders is an essential part of the job. If the project has a steep focus on analytics, then at least some Data Science training should be required.

- Programming Language: If hiring for a technical role, you will want your team to have at least one to two programming languages under the belt. Because of the dependency on databases, SQL programming is a must. Your ETL tool may have additional programming requirements such as Java or JavaScript, but that rests clearly with the chosen software.

- Software: Your project is driven by an in-house ETL tool, either existing or up for grabs. Make sure the person you hire has experience with a specific application or some semblance of one. It does not have to be a precise 1:1 match as one software product may have transferable functionality to another. What matters most is that the candidate knows the terminology and can talk about the approach for architecting/developing a design.

- Operating System: Some hiring managers focus more on the software and language than the operating system, but this skill is an excellent predictor of how fast new team members will be able to hit the ground running. If your shop leans toward a Windows environment, then state that. If Mac dependent, then go that way. What matters is that you interview people who already have training in the particular platform you use. I've encountered many people with fantastic integration skills who did not understand simple Unix shell commands. The curve can be steep when simultaneously learning new software on unfamiliar operating systems, so keep this in mind when writing your job description.

- Language: By this, I mean native and secondary language fluency. As mentioned earlier, communication among the team is critical, even with your more technical back-end roles, which may have a last-minute update during deployment. If you need fluent speakers and writers in a particular language, then call that out.

An excellent place to start thinking about your description is `https://work.chron.com/job-description-etl-developer-26435.html`.[25] Various sites across the Web will have other alternatives as well.

Finding Candidates

Once you have a clear understanding of what you need, where do you go to find the best pool of candidates? There are two main avenues to explore:

- Internal to your organization
- External to your organization

Internal Candidates

If you work for an organization where roles are loosely defined, the integration project itself is a short-term supplemental, or if you are just beginning to build your integration practice, you may be able to find some interested candidates within your current software development or IT team. The main advantage of going this route is that you can establish a pipeline early on as those qualified individuals who want to take on additional responsibilities and who will let you know this path as soon as you announce the project. The second advantage of internal hiring is that you can assess your candidates based on their peers' recommendations—you will be able to evaluate those who fit the role better than an unknown source. Of course, if you require a different degree of skills than what is available within the organization, you will have to reach out externally.

---

[25]"Job Description for an ETL Developer." 2019. *Work.chron.com*. `https://work.chron.com/job-description-etl-developer-26435.html`

External Candidates

Referrals

One of the best ways to find qualified external candidates is the same as the route of evaluating internal candidates: referrals. In this case, getting leads from your top hires is by asking about their favorite past coworkers. This method probably works more than any other, so much so that one study found that 46% of hires at top-performing companies came from internal referral sources.[26] The reason referrals are great at finding candidates may not be monetarily related (it is questionable whether employee referral bonuses work,[27] but rather more a function of people knowing their associates' personalities, likes, and dislikes).

Although a referral program may land you some good leads, it is not the only method. The following are a few others you might want to consider.

Outsourcing

Earlier, we talked about hiring independent contractors for placing on short-term projects. If you need extra horsepower, want specialized skills, or want a different perspective on your internal culture, bringing in a consulting team with specializations in data warehousing, data integration, or anything with the words "data" and "migration" in it might be the way to go.[28] Again, this might only be a quick fix for a much lengthier initiative that needs full-time commitment, but—if you are willing to outsource your team to a third party and don't mind footing the bill—it does substitute for direct employee support.

---

[26]"Why Employee Referrals Are The Best Source Of Hire". 2019. *Undercover Recruiter*. https://theundercoverrecruiter.com/infographic-employee-referrals-hire/.

[27]See, e.g., "How to Implement an Employee Referral Bonus | Workable." 2019. *Recruiting Resources: How to Recruit and Hire Better*. https://resources.workable.com/tutorial/employee-referral-bonus

[28]"Good to Know: Why Companies Really Hire Consultants." 2019. *Themuse.com*. www.themuse.com/advice/good-to-know-why-companies-really-hire-consultants

Posting to Job Boards

Posting to a job board is probably the number one method for companies with do-it-yourself recruiting, and it does have its strengths. But there is also a bit of effort from your end to ensure the various applicants truly fit the role and haven't exaggerated on their resume. We advise that you post your jobs to multiple locations and to the ones that have good reputations for vetting their candidates. There are a lot of free posting sites with which you can start. Try `www.betterteam.com/job-posting-sites`[29] for a list of popular ones and see where your first posts will lead.

Hiring a Recruiter

Finding candidates can be a lengthy, time-consuming process. Rather than you doing the work, hiring a recruiter who will do it for you may be a better use of your time. They will post job descriptions to online boards, go through social media outlets, and arrange the next steps in the interview process.[30] If you do decide to go this route, make sure you precisely cover the job descriptions and the required skills with the recruiter. Too often, I have heard of recruiters who perform mass mailings for job descriptions on LinkedIn, returning with a list of semiqualified candidates and then following up with them with only a partial explanation of what the organization meant. Four out of five times, this occurs because the organization did not know either. Simply stated, when working with a recruiter, be clear and precise on the type of integration skills and qualifications you need and check in often for status updates and clarifications.

Networking

Attending career fairs and showing up at recruiting events are other ways to find qualified job leads. This practice is solid advice to follow even when the position is not available yet but could be in the future. The person you meet today could be a top hire in the future, and keeping in touch with them can lead to many potential opportunities for them as well as your organization.

---

[29]"19 Free Job Posting Sites—High Traffic and 100% Free." 2019. *Betterteam.* `www.betterteam.com/job-posting-sites`

[30]Blakely-Gray, Rachel. 2019. "Sourcing Candidates | How Do Recruiters Find Candidates?" *Top Echelon.* `www.topechelon.com/blog/recruiter-training/sourcing-candidates-how-do-recruiters-find-candidates/`

Conducting Interviews

One of the last significant steps in hiring for your team is the interview process. Due to the many books available on this theme,[31] I will not cover the basics in any detail. I will add, however, that finding the perfect integration expert—that is, the correct balance of extroversion and introversion, back-end coder and front-end conversationalist, documenter, leader, and overall innovator—may be tough to ascertain in a 45-minute interview. Rather than going through the standard rote material (I am partial to "Where do you see yourself five years from now?"), you use your time to clarify the ETL technologies with which the applicant has worked, the integration-specific problems they have resolved, and any unique talents or traits which may be useful for the team and organization in general.

If you are on the fence with a particular candidate—that is, you like them but are unsure that they possess the right skills—then I have two rules of thumb:

- Go with your gut.

- Look for passion. You can learn any technique with the right medium, but only passion will keep you in the game. That is especially true for integration projects where a single misstep can lead to hours of thankless correction. If you see that spark of excitement in your candidate, then run with it.

Summary

And there you have it. We've covered a lot about building the integration team within this chapter, and there's probably more we can go over, but we will have to save that for a later date. Let's consider what we've learned:

- Team Personality: Each member of the integration team should be willing to communicate and to code on an equal basis.

- Types of Teams: There are four types of teams we discussed— functional, cross-functional, virtual, and self-directed. Although each one has a place in data integration, the most common type will be cross-functional.

---

[31]E.g., "Amazon Best Sellers: Best Job Interviewing." 2019. *Amazon.com*. www.amazon.com/Best-Sellers-Books-Job-Interviewing/zgbs/books/2578

- Team Sizes: Waterfall team sizes will be large, agile team sizes will be small. Depending on the integration project, we will have to measure based on our needs, although two to five will suffice in the beginning.

- Agile and Waterfall Team Expectations: Agile skill expectations are wide, waterfall skill expectations are deep. Ideally, you will want T-shaped people.

- Integration Team Roles: An integration team is like a software development team with three fundamental differences in terms of a lead (data integration architect), developers (ETL), and business analyst (integration focused). As a reminder, the project manager still owns the plan, and the product owner still owns the application. The technical team owns the integration *process*.

- Recruiting Your Team: We discussed the job description, how to find qualified candidates both within and outside the organization, and tips for interviewing.

Now that we have an integration team, a project plan, and customers ready for us to get started, it's time for us to get our hands dirty. In the next chapter, we talk about documentation and its importance in the realm of integration.

CHAPTER 4

Finding Your Purpose: Project Deliverables

Things of quality have no fear of time.

—Author Unknown

Introduction

Now that your integration team is in place, the actual project can begin. The goal here, of course, is to complete a set of tasks to ensure that the data moves successfully from one point to another, be it one time, daily, or multiple times throughout the day. You can measure your success in this effort in a variety of different ways: Did you meet the client's business needs? Does the data flow in a "reasonable" amount of time (where you know the value of "reasonable")? Does the integration run as expected, or are there exceptions that must be abided? If so, who is responsible for resolving? Is the documentation of the process and code clear and complete? With all these success factors, you will no doubt forget some critical detail, and someone, somewhere, is going to be upset. And that brings us to the topic of this chapter: ensuring your success through project deliverables.

Having well-defined deliverables is just a shortcut to maintain your sanity. Overkill is easy with integration primarily because with all the data available now, and in the future, stakeholders are never sure where to draw the line; there is always something more to move, always some obscure anomaly in a legacy database that people want to embed in the new system. For that reason, no one ever really wants to sign off and say enough is enough. I've been on many projects where the answer to "what data should we move" is the very nonspecific "everything." Not coincidentally, these requirements tend to be the same projects where the project sponsors expect the integration to take one long weekend.

49

J. Goldfedder, *Building a Data Integration Team*, https://doi.org/10.1007/978-1-4842-5653-4_4

With that in mind, documenting and sharing plans with others and letting them know what features to expect from start to finish is the best approach. Otherwise, stakeholders may push back and claim that they absolutely must have more than can be possibly delivered in the time allotted. With the right documentation, you create a robust framework which keeps everyone confident and on the same page. More importantly, it helps you get to bed at a reasonable time.

Project Management Phases

Documents are produced and delivered throughout the project lifecycle, whether working in a waterfall or an agile model. The types of materials are relatively the same, just occurring in a more clipped, more accelerated pace with the agile framework. Before we discuss the specifics of each deliverable, however, let's begin our conversation with the phases of project management and how they map directly to your integration process.

Some articles have highlighted six phases of project management processes, some have described four,[1] while the definitive guide, the PMBOK, asserts there are five.[2] From my experience, teams usually stick with whatever the organization itself traditionally follows. In any case, we'll go with the idea that more is better than less, and discuss the six phases. You can omit whatever you think is necessary for your project based on its perceived simplicity or complexity and determine how to compose the framework of your integration team.

The phases of project management are as follows:

- Initiation

- Definition

- Design

- Development

- Implementation

- Maintenance

---

[1]"Project Management Life Cycle Phases | Lucidchart." 2019. *Lucidchart.com*. www.lucidchart.com/blog/the-4-phases-of-the-project-management-life-cycle

[2]"The PMBOK'S Five Project Phases." 2019. *Projectengineer*. www.projectengineer.net/the-pmboks-five-project-phases/

Initiation

The initiation phase is the beginning of the project in which team planners first vet the ideas and consider the project feasibility. They make decisions as to who will carry out the project, what teams will be involved, and how important the project is to the organization as a whole.

It is at this phase that the proposal is written to secure executive financing. It is also the riskiest phase where misunderstandings can occur as the developers believe they are delivering a prototype while the stakeholders are expecting a working model. Clarification is key.

Definition

The definition phase is sometimes also called the discovery phase in which the requirements that are associated with a project result are specified as clearly as possible ("discovered"). This phase reconfirms the expectations that all team members have on the final product by establishing functional versus nonfunctional measurements.[3] The list of questions for this phase can go on and on, and somewhere, amid the noise, the requirements for migration/integration will also be hammered out. Depending on the level of technical complexity, gathering these particular requirements should be the responsibility of either the business analyst or the integration lead who has an eye focused on understanding the business requirements.

Design Phase

The design phase is the next step in which the development teams use the requirements from the definition phase to make design decisions that move the project toward a successful result. To do this, the teams inspect and consider various models ranging from dioramas, sketches, flowcharts, site trees, HTML screen designs, prototypes, photo impressions, and UML schemas.[4] Once the final design is chosen, implementation can begin.

---

[3]For definitions and examples of functional and nonfunctional, see Eriksson, Ulf. 2019. "Functional Requirements vs. Nonfunctional Requirements." *Reqtest.* https://reqtest.com/requirements-blog/functional-vs-non-functional-requirements/

[4]"Design Phase—Projectmanagement-Training.Net." 2019. *Projectmanagement-training.net.* www.projectmanagement-training.net/design-phase/

Development

Development is one of those phases that may or may not be formalized depending on the size of the project—in other words, smaller projects combine "development" with the implementation phase into what we call "execution." Nevertheless, it is worth discussing since it occasionally has importance with implementation projects.

From the project management standpoint, the development phase arranges everything needed for project implementation. Planners bring in the suppliers and contractors, make schedules, order software and equipment, and provide personnel with additional instructions. At some point, teams will be ready to implement and will close the development phase.

Implementation

The implementation phase is where the actual project construction occurs. Developers code, teams hold their status meetings, and an actual build is taking place. Outsiders become aware that changes are happening and may even take place in demonstrations and proof-of-concept prototypes. It is here that work is happening, and teams are busy collaborating, testing, and eventually deploying their product.

The most significant measure of success for evaluating the implementation phase is determining how well the product meets the expectations of definition phase requirements and whether the problem faced by the business is solved. Design also plays an important aspect; if the code only works occasionally due to system complexity, then the model may have been flawed, and some redesign may be necessary. The point is that "success" is a highly subjective perspective and that only by answering the question "Are we better now than before?" can a confident declaration be made.

This impression does not negate the fact that despite our best efforts, we may not meet project requirements in the final product. This failure can occur for several reasons: the requirements changed from definition to implementation, miscommunications occurred due to high expectations, or teams underestimated the level of effort by falsely assuming they could complete work by a specific time. More than likely, multiple culprits exist and will eagerly be broken down into further detail by managers, developers, and stakeholders, usually discussed in confidentiality over drinks. I think the famous Tree Swing, as shown in Figure 4-1, represents these expectations best.

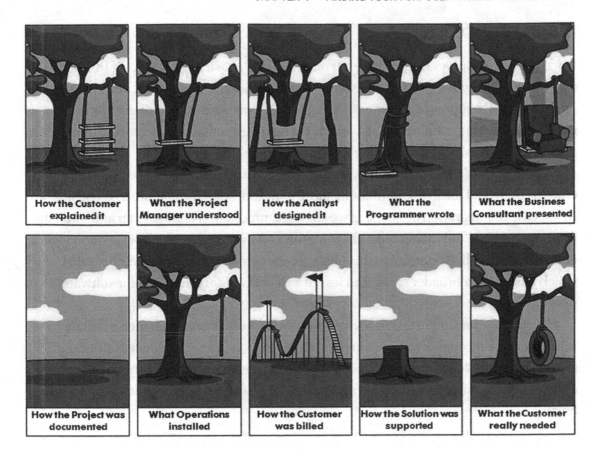

Figure 4-1. How IT Projects Really Work[5]

We can minimize these potentials for failure in various ways. For example, the Agile manifesto covers 12 principles designed to do so.[6] But it is not always so easy to put these theories into practice, and sometimes hindsight seems to be the best teacher, albeit a tough one.

Later in the chapter, we will discuss how to use the proper documentation to minimize errors within your integration plan.

---

[5]Possel, Heiko. 2019. "How IT Projects Really Work." Smart-jokes.org. www.smart-jokes.org/how-it-projects-really-work.html

[6]"12 Principles Behind the Agile Manifesto | Agile Alliance." 2019. *Agile Alliance.* www.agilealliance.org/agile101/12-principles-behind-the-agile-manifesto/

Maintenance

Once the team deploys the product, the maintenance phase begins. During this phase, everything is arranged that is necessary to bring to close the project and keep the system operational.[7] Examples of activities in this phase include writing handbooks and user guides, conducting training classes, setting up help desk support, monitoring the results, and formally delivering the product to its final owner.

As simple as these activities may sound, it is tough to know when the project truly ends, as there will always be something more to fix and something more to reconsider. In the case of integration projects, as we shall see, production changes can and often do go above and beyond maintenance as the team and users discover new exception logic. For this reason, I like referring to this phase as operations and maintenance (O&M), which has a much broader scope and less of a clear boundary than regular software development.

The main intention of this model allows its members to plan, act, then evaluate. Whether done through a waterfall methodology (plan, act, evaluate once) or through an agile methodology (plan, act, evaluate, plan, act, evaluate, repeat as necessary), the output in each phase should be the same: to produce essential milestones from start to finish.[8]

Integration Milestones

When it comes to the integration part of the project, what matters most is the communication among the architects, designers, and stakeholders. A missed requirement or inaccurate transformation will not only delay system completion but—should the transfer of data fail—could cause a great deal of damage, not just locally but on a global level. One famous incident is the Black Monday Stock Market Crash of 1987, in which the massive exchange of data allegedly caused a cascading effect, forcing all bids simultaneously to vanish around the stock market. According to some experts, the

---

[7]"Follow Up Phase—Projectmanagement-Training.Net." 2019. *Projectmanagement-training.net.* www.projectmanagement-training.net/follow-up-phase/

[8]"Project Management Life Cycle Phases | Lucidchart." 2019. *Lucidchart.com.* www.lucidchart.com/blog/the-4-phases-of-the-project-management-life-cycle

computer systems had not been tested on how to handle market orders during a crash.[9] Just based on this one event, understanding the integration process and its potential pitfalls should be paramount for all concerned.

But, as we have discussed, that is not always the case. During the project management phases, planners often treat the integration tasks as just another part of software development. A functional requirement such as "the system should move contact first name, last name, postal code, and phone number from database X into database Y" is all well and good from the 30,000-foot view, but it doesn't necessarily cover the unacceptable scenario of what happens when the phone number or zip code values use different formats (see Chapter 5). If not encountered and dealt with early in the project phases, the integration—hence the system itself—will fail.

This now brings us to the integration milestones. These milestones occur side by side with the software delivery phases but require distinct outputs. Table 4-1 provides a summary of the distinct project phases, the phase gate deliverables, and a brief description.

Table 4-1. *Project Phase and Migration Documents*

Project Phase	Phase Gate Deliverable	Description
Initiation	Team Representation	Inclusion of one or more integration team representatives to confirm or negate any assumptions associated with delivering project proposals.
Definition	Data Migration Plan	Documents project background and purpose, migration and integration approach, assumptions, constraints, risks, as well as current and future state architecture.
Design	Data Profile Analysis	Review of source data, structure, content, and relationships for content and quality.
Design	Issues Log	Records and tracks any issues or questions related to data quality and data migration.

(*continued*)

---

[9]"What Caused Black Monday: The Stock Market Crash Of 1987?" 2019. *Investopedia.* www.investopedia.com/ask/answers/042115/what-caused-black-monday-stock-market-crash-1987.asp

Table 4-1. (*continued*)

Project Phase	Phase Gate Deliverable	Description
Design	Source-to-Target Mapping	Documents mapping from source to target, including data types and transformation rules.
Design	Data Migration Process Flow Design	Documents detailed design for migration processes, including the order of operations.
Development	ETL Scripts	Documents the front- and back-end code related to the extraction, transformation, and loading; should be followed up with peer review session.
Implementation	Migration Results Report	Documents migration results by object, breakdown, and impact of errors, action items, and risks. The report is created after each migration, including mock/test migrations.
Implementation	Go-Live/Deployment Plan	Documents detailed, step-by-step, start-to-finish plan to perform the migration, including dependencies.

We will discuss each one of these deliverables in depth. For now, I want to stress that this pattern of delivery is not mandatory. It is merely one way to achieve the goal inherent in any collaborative endeavor; that is, it weakens (and even avoids) the impact when stakeholders realize that the meal they will get is different from what they thought they ordered. It also makes the life of the development team easier as most questions are covered from the get-go rather than at the last minute when the amount of work suddenly reveals itself to be larger than "just a weekend of button-pushing."

Initiation

The secret to getting behind the complexity of integration is involvement from the very beginning, and this means representation at the earliest phase of project initiation. For traditional managers, it may seem strange to have straight technical representation included in a business proposal, but false assumptions and misunderstandings happen all the time, skewing the understanding of scope and effort. For one thing, organizations tend to reuse proposal boilerplate that has worked for them in the past. That makes sense from a repeatability standpoint—a process of delivery would be the same for similar products. But if we keep in mind that integrations are meant to be unique, then we realize how important it is to make sure we cover all bases concerning this process. That is, just because a particular source-to-target architecture worked in the past does not mean it translates equally well to a similar type of project. The data stored in Database A for a client does not equal the same data stored in Database B for another client. Customizations, triggers, values, and everything else that needs migration require a full profile analysis, and this must be taken into account when thinking about our product.

An integration team representative should be asked their well-grounded opinion on the viability, expected time, and effort with a particular migration piece. And although we should not be discussing technical solutions at this point, at the very least, the questions "How complicated will this be?" and "How much staff will you need?" should be part of the proposal's arsenal of discussion. If the answers to technical questions are still mostly unknown, then that should be stated. The point is that the proposal should reflect the unknowns rather than make an outright risky (or inaccurate!) assumption based on past projects.

In short, including an integration representative in the proposal creates an accurate plan and ensures that a timeboxed solution is viable. It also builds confidence that the project is achievable without too many fires breaking out due to unannounced expectations.

Definition

Integration requirements tend to be either highly specific (i.e., "we only want these three fields brought in unless the user is from the account department, in which case we only should be using these other three fields") or not specific enough (i.e., "we want everything"). For this reason, and to avoid the overwhelming flood of requests that can happen on a first iteration, it is essential to build a checklist of functional and nonfunctional requirements that should be a part of a document called the Data Migration Plan. This document provides in some detail the project background and purpose, the migration and integration approach, assumptions, constraints, risks, as well as current and future state architecture.

Data Migration Plan

The Appendix contains a Data Migration Plan template along with definitions of sample sections to include. As with all templates, you can structure the model to whatever fits your own organization's needs, keeping in mind that its purpose is consistent. You are communicating a solution, gaining consensus that your assumptions are correct, and setting expectations of what the team will deliver as a final product.

The topics in the Data Migration Plan include the following:

- Overview: The background of the project, usually copied from the proposal or other project management plans. This section also should contain at least one or two paragraphs on the goals of the current migration/integration tasks and how it meets the overall business objectives.

- Assumptions, Constraints, Risks, and Gaps: This section sets the expectations for the limits of the current project, preventing the "I want everything" syndrome we identified in a previous chapter. In it, we define some of what our team can and cannot do versus what other teams must do (assumptions), limitations due to technology or time (constraints), potential issues that might occur (risks), and areas of the implementation that remain an open source of debate (gaps). These details are highly relevant throughout the project, especially when producing results that are either in or out of our area of influence.

- Architecture: This section contains two broad constructs—the current state and the future state. The current state represents the "as-is" system, that is, where the data currently rests, the data systems involved, the counts of records stored, and other details that would help teammates familiarize themselves with the existing data model. The future state is the "to-be" system—the final snapshot where the data will exist after the project is complete. Its subcategories would include parallel topics to the current state, but with more of an assumptive flavor (where the data will rest, the data systems that will be involved, expected counts, and so on). Since much of the future state will be unknown at the outset, it is more of an ideal world with gaps that you will answer in as you continue to gather requirements.

Note   Special attention should be paid to the development tools as well. These will be the technologies we are building with (e.g., Python, Java, .NET) as well as specialized software related to the build, DevOps, and ETL.

- Data Migration Approach: This section covers the overall approach to the integration, such as scope, roles, and responsibilities of team members; what should take place pre-, during, and post-migration; and contingency plans should the whole system fall apart. These requirements should be regarded as brushstrokes of possibilities within a larger painting. The real details will be highlighted later in the design phase when reality hits home. For now, you should focus on what you can accomplish that will best meet the user's expectations. If you find blockers along the way, then you can always backtrack or figure out alternative routes to achieve the same purpose.

- Testing/Validation: Testing and Validation is one of the more important topics in migration, but also the one that receives the least amount of attention. One reason may be that the developers who write their code may not be very good at testing it.[10] Nevertheless, it is important that we have a solid framework in mind on how to test our integrations and that we document it in the Data Migration Plan. We should include the type of tests we plan to conduct (unit testing, joint integration, verification testing, and so on). We should also describe the kinds of environments we will use for testing and which teams will be conducting the tests. As with the Data Migration Approach, we will not have all the answers, but we can fill in as many blanks as possible to get a fair estimate.

---

[10]Montvelisky, Joel. 2019. "Why Developers Are Poor Testers and What to Do About It?" *Simple Programmer.* https://simpleprogrammer.com/developers-poor-testers-can-done/

The Discovery Process: Tips and Tricks

As far as the actual discovery process, there is much more to describe than we can cover here. If you want a good book on agile requirements gathering, check out Jeff Patton's book *User Story Mapping* (2014).[11] In terms of integration mapping, the following are a few tips that will make your sessions more effective.

Learn the Architecture

Because you may be working across multiple systems and silos, understanding the current architecture as quickly as possible is mandatory. To do this, you must reach out to the people who best understand the back-end data. Find and review any Entity Relationship Diagrams (ERDs) you come across. Learn about the nature of the business and how the future model should look. Ask good questions (to get you started, *http://www.etlsolutions.com/data-migration-planning-checklist/* covers a process-driven and tactical checklist of points).

Keep Your Session Small

Contrary to the opinions of program directors I have worked with, I often find that the smaller the group, the better the collaboration. I would say that, on average, a one-on-one requirements gathering session lasting two hours tends to cover more ground than an entire team sitting for a half-day session, and much of this has to do with *focus*. It is very easy during these sessions to go off the rails—one person says a requirement, another person disagrees, a third person corrects the first two, and so on. By the time the session is over, there are a dozen open topics with almost no accompanying resolution.

The same outcome rarely happens when conducting a single-person interview. The primary advice on going this route, to paraphrase former US President Ronald Reagan, is to "trust but verify."[12] Take the requirements as stated, write them down, add them to your Data Migration Plan, and then share them with the rest of the stakeholders during a phase review. If it is an obvious error, someone with a strong opinion will correct it. If not, there is always the chance that someone will identify it as such in future phases. The point here is that it is much easier to correct the stated flow of words than the unstated flow of thoughts.

---

[11]"*User Story Mapping*—Jeff Patton & Associates." 2019. *Jeff Patton & Associates*. www.jpattonassociates.com/user-story-mapping/

[12]"Leadergrow: Articles by Robert Whipple, the Trust Ambassador—Trust but Verify." 2019. *Leadergrow.com*. www.leadergrow.com/articles/443-trust-but-verify

Get System Access Early

You're going to need access to systems, potentially lots of them like servers, databases, files, hidden directories, and the like. Get permission to use these systems as soon as you can. Having them available during your discovery session will help illustrate the point that your discussion counterpart is trying to make. It also helps end the debate much faster when you prove that the file that is supposed to be a qualified list of customers is actually a list of championship apple pie recipes (I'm not kidding, this really did happen on one of my assignments).

Design

With the first iteration of requirements complete, it's now time to start the design phase. This phase represents the moment when the technical team pulls away from the business side of the house and begins to code the solution, identifying issues through data analysis, peer review, and program debugging. Consequently, it is also the phase where the most amount of documentation, hence written communication, is produced. As with the Data Migration Plan from the previous phase, design templates are available in the Appendix.

We'll now discuss each document to elaborate on the basic framework.

Data Profile Analysis

We have access to the source systems and a full dataset supplied for our review. But how clean, valid, and reliable is the data with which we are working? To answer, we must first conduct a Data Profile Analysis, the process of reviewing source data; understanding the structure, content, and interrelationships; and then identifying their potential for data projects.[13]

What we're interested in here is whether the source data we are analyzing is going to move cleanly into our target system. For instance, let's say you have 20,000 contact records to move. Only 25% of them, or 5,000, contain a street address. The new system, however, will *require* this street address to be included upon insertion. In other words, without doing anything, you're going to have 15,000 records omitted from the new system. What should you do?

---

[13]"What Is Data Profiling? Process, Best Practices and Tools." 2019. *Panoply.* https://panoply.io/analytics-stack-guide/data-profiling-best-practices/

You can probably come up with several solutions:

1. Put a default value of "N/A" on the source system's street addresses that are blank.

2. Allow the target system to temporarily accept NULL values and then turn back on the constraint after your initial migration is complete.

3. Inform the business that someone must populate these records in the source.

Each one of these options requires a specific level of effort, and you must work with teams to decide before performing any migrations. Exposing these issues and their workarounds is the primary purpose of the Data Profile Analysis.

I've seen many talented analysts fall apart on this deliverable. What data fundamentals matter, and what should be omitted? One suggestion is to include these topics:

- Collecting descriptive statistics like min, max, count, and sum

- Collecting data types, length, and recurring patterns

- Tagging data with keywords, descriptions, or categories

- Performing data quality assessment, risk of performing joins on the data

- Discovering metadata and assessing its accuracy

- Identifying distributions, key candidates, foreign-key candidates, functional dependencies, and embedded value dependencies and performing inter-table analysis

It seems complicated for the novice, and it may be. Fortunately, we don't need to reinvent the wheel as there are a number of both open source and third-party tools available for use.[14] One of the ones I have recommended for many years is Don McMunn's Freeware Data Profiling Tool Kit at *http://www.ipcdesigns.com/data_profiling/*. It provides a series of queries for SQL Server and Oracle that create data profiling tables that you can then incorporate with your datasets. At the very least, it offers a guide for standard data profiling fields you may want to include in your analysis.

---

[14]Valcheva, Silvia. 2019. "Best Data Profiling Tools and Software Solutions: List." *Business Intelligence, Data Science, and Management*. http://intellspot.com/data-profiling-tools/

Remember, having even a small subset of profiled data is better than reviewing nothing at all.

Issues Log

Inevitably, you will see something along your data design journey that was never discussed during requirements gathering. It may be an isolated field or a table of data that is ripe for the new target but remains unidentified. You will have questions and require further clarification. To keep track of this, we recommend storing your comments in an Issues Log, a document that records and tracks issues or questions related to the data quality and data migration process. Keep this file in a physical notebook, a thumb drive file, or, better yet, a group folder online where teams can review and provide immediate feedback. Whatever way you choose to store the information, make sure you direct the right question to the right team members and, more importantly, get the answers you need.

Source-to-Target Mapping

If there's one thing you take away from this book, it's the importance of properly maintaining a Source-to-Target mapping (STTM) spreadsheet. This document is the end all, be all of integration and, consequently, a mandatory part of the process. No excuses for skipping this part, so read and reread this section until it becomes rote.

Because the STTM is such a critical component, I will go into more detail on its purpose, design, and usage than in other sections. Hopefully, by the end of the reading, you'll have a clear understanding of why this deliverable matters so much.

Purpose

The Source-to-Target mapping is "a set of data transformation structures that determine how to covert the structure and content of data in the source system to the structure and content needed in the target."[15] In short, it is your playlist of requirements for extracting, transforming, and then reloading your data. Think of it as a roadmap of expected inputs and outputs, with the step-by-step transformation in the middle.

---

[15]"What Is Source-to-Target Mapping? | Knowledge Center | Lore IO." 2019. *Getlore.io.*
   www.getlore.io/knowledgecenter/source-to-target-mapping

Design

Shown in the following is the *minimal* amount of information you will need for your STTM spreadsheet:

- Source Datasystem: The generic or formal name of the system that serves as the source, for example, `Oracle` or, if by official organization title, `Legacy Contact Management System`

- Source Table: The physical name of the source table, for example, CONTACT

- Source Field: The physical name of the source field/column, for example, "`Name`", "`Email`", or "`Street Address`"

- Target Datasystem: The generic or formal name of the system that serves as the target, for example, `Salesforce` or, if by official organization title, `Payroll Management System`

- Target Table: The physical name of the target table, for example, `EMPLOYEE__C`

- Target Field: The physical name of the target field/column, for example, "`Name__c`", "`Email__c`", or "`street_address_1__c`"

- Transformation Rule: The business rules required for transforming the data from the source field to the target field, for example, "`Join contact_id on payroll__c and add rowid where address.primary_address = TRUE and address.valid=TRUE`"

A template illustrating this pattern is in the Appendix.

If this design sounds relatively simple, think again. I've met many database experts who, thinking they had mapped their sources and targets with single-phrase transformation sentences, regret their decisions months later when they needed to reference this information. The important thing to keep in mind is specificity and keeping information current. If you need to have lengthy details, then feel free to do so in a separate document, perhaps with a hyperlink in the Transformation Rules with something to the effect of "See document XXX for more details." Make sure, above all else, that the document makes sense to the readers. Don't get too technical or wordy as this document most likely will be your legacy after you close up shop and leave or, more optimistically, delegate to others after you win the lottery and spend the remainder of your working years sipping Mai Tais on the beach.

Even with the provided information, however, you may still not have enough. Of course, you're going to modify your business requirements at some point, and new tables and fields may need to be added as you continue analyzing and finding more data points. Note that we're not talking about *versioning*, which is overwriting the STTM in place and replacing it with the latest version. We're talking about *tracking*, which is making changes and then justifying why you made those changes. Consider these optional fields that could be included alongside the basic STTM:

- Design Notes: Additional notes not necessarily part of the transformation rules but still crucial for history, for example, "changed this field from fullname to lastname due to client request."

- Date Created: The datetime the record was initially added to the model (e.g., 9/14/2019). Once inserted, this value does not change.

- Date Updated: The datetime any part of the record was modified. This value, when associated with Design Notes, will help you maintain the historical tracking.

Now we're getting somewhere. By adding these three descriptors, we can document any changes made to the STTM along with the date of origin and update. The key here, of course, is having robust design notes which, depending on the reasons for the change, may get quite bulky in length—new notes can always be appended on top, separating from the old notes with a semicolon (";"). Better yet, you can always add a "See document xxx" reference. Modifying the Date Updated field may seem like a minor inconvenience, but it is something that, once you get used to, is relatively easy to follow up. Tip: If using Microsoft Excel or Access, select a cell and hold down the control key (CTRL) plus semicolon (;) get the current date. Similarly, hold down the control key (CTRL) plus colon (:) to get the current time.

There are other columns you may want to include on the STTM, and I have included them as part of the template located in the Appendix. One in particular that I've seen is "DataType" for both the source and target, for example, "VARCHAR(80)", "DATETIME", "NUMBER", or any other plethora of data. I often do not include these values as this is more of a fixed schema design; you can look on any Entity Relationship Diagram to see them, so I don't quite get the purpose. Still, you may want to include them for either the source or target if you frequently need to use your STTM spreadsheet to lookup values of a particular type such as primary keys denoted with, say, an "ID" on "NUMBER."

Usage

As we have seen, the STTM spreadsheet serves the role of not just a design tool, but also a reference for later review and, perhaps most importantly, a reminder on the decisions made. While in the throes of testing a project, stakeholders dealing with multiple issues may forget why they asked for a specific field or why they changed from Table X to Table Y three months prior. The STTM fields "Design Notes" and "Date Updated" will quickly settle the matter. I cannot tell you how often we turn back to the STTM, days, months, or even years after a project ends. That is why it is essential to keep the deliverable close, keeping it updated with the current model and making it accessible to all through either a shared drive or even an online database repository that allows for fast, convenient lookup when the system starts to crash and all eyes turn to the integration team for answers.

Data Migration Process Flow Design

This document, part of the design process, summarizes the detailed design for migration processes, including the order of operations that are to take place on the one-time migration and daily updates. It is a repository for the other deliverables that are part of the overall strategy and allows teams to communicate the proposed approach for project success. As with the other deliverables we have discussed, it too is a *living* document, always changing and available for updates.

Order of Operations

The Order of Operations discusses the high-level step-by-step operations for object migration in general. This section breaks down into more detail for the "Deployment Steps" described later. I like to include illustrations whenever possible as they are more descriptive and comprehensive than just words alone.

Mapping Logic

The Mapping Logic defines the high-level rules behind the Source-to-Target Mapping spreadsheet, mostly for business teams to confirm that the rules are accurate. Note that this is not a rehashing of the entire STTM (see section "Source-to-Target Mapping") but, at most, just a few of the more essential fields that get the fundamental points of the integration across to stakeholders and executives. At a minimum, include a link to your STTM spreadsheet or repository with instructions on how to use it (browsers required, tools needed, and so on) and under what circumstances.

Deployment Steps

A deeper dive into the Order of Operations, the Deployment Steps section defines each task of the migration or integration, usually with a diagram associated with the ETL process. The pattern should be easy to follow and essentially becomes the checklist of the deployment cycle:

1. Select data from table XXX:

   ```
   Transform data with defined business requirements
   Test sample
   Insert data into table YYY
   ```

   And then, each of these tasks is further broken down into a single-sentence summary of steps.

2. Select data from table XXX:

   a. Using the Pentaho Data Integration (PDI) application, run SQL statements against table XXX via a SQL Server connection located here.

3. Transform data with defined business requirements:

   a. Using Python script, transform Salesforce contact data into provided business rules.

4. Test sample:

   a. Insert ten sample contact records into Preproduction environment ensuring that five to ten sample records are successfully received.

   b. Perform QA assessment of data. If records fail or do not meet business requirements, then iterate and reload.

   c. Insert data into table YYY.

   d. Once test records pass, receive Go/No Go permission from stakeholders.

5.   Perform a load of the entire dataset using Talend ETL application:

   a. Once the load is complete, confirm the load is successful against contact record by performing follow-up analysis.

   b. If the load fails, roll back transaction and report error to stakeholders.

6.   Reiterate and restart from Step 1.

The beautiful thing about this part of the Data Migration Flow document is that you are preparing for most of the eventualities before they can even happen. Sure, you may miss one or two things, but knowing that this is an adjustable document that you can always modify and append makes your life much easier. If you stage a few dress rehearsal migrations in a development or sandbox environment, you'll be able to catch most everything that will occur during the actual deployments. That, and you'll have the written confidence that you knew well in advance what you wanted to do, how you would do it, and the conditions that will occur based on success or failure. No one will ever be able to come back to you and claim they were surprised. So it may require a bit of up-front work, but I think that this level of preparation and communication is well worth the effort.

Log File Delivery

This section describes where the success and error logs will be stored. This storage location can be online or emailed as a shared file, but it should be available to those who have need and interest in seeing results.

Migration Results

The Migration Results section describes the output received by the Migration Results Report, which we discuss later. In truth, I usually leave this section empty until the end of the project, using it as gift wrapping to prove that data was delivered as expected. It is also a signal to the team that with all records successfully delivered, final signoff is imminent.

Final Signoff

Not mandatory, but I like to include this part of the Data Migration Process Flow as it gives closure to your migration. As the name implies, signoff is either an email or attachment, signed by the project sponsor, that the migration was completed and satisfied the requirements. You may be shaking your head in disbelief as you read that last sentence, but I promise you, with the process documentation we have in place, you will end up meeting the project requirements. And be organized and prepared while doing it.

ETL Scripts

The ETL scripts are part of the development phase and, because they are highly technical, may not be a critical part of the overall delivery. Still, it is always nice to have a copy of your code stored just in case the backups should crash or some other tragedy befalls your local platform.

You must consider a variety of possibilities for how you want to document and deliver your functionality. The development team should hold peer reviews frequently, and having some troublesome script logic in hand during these sessions can be helpful to get everyone on board. Plus, sharing your approach with more junior ETL developers will be beneficial as they align your ideas against their projects.

Capturing this information may be a simple cut-and-paste against data, but most of the more popular ETL tools use both graphical interfaces and text. In this case, a screenshot tool may do the trick (my favorites include Microsoft's Snipping Tool [*https://support.microsoft.com/en-us/help/13776/windows-10-use-snipping-tool-to-capture-screenshots*], TechSmith's Snagit [*https://www.techsmith.com/screen-capture.html*], or NGWIN's PicPick [*https://picpick.app/en/*]). In some cases, you may be able to pull out snippets of GUI code through configuration files, but I leave it to readers to decide what will work best. The most important thing to keep in mind is that code, like any other iterable software product, forever changes and that whatever you document will ultimately need to be updated.

Migration Results Report

This deliverable, populated during integration, highlights the success and error counts of the integration for each object. You'll have to keep track of your load statistics, be it through manually written notes, an automated email, or another type of delivery that tracks the number of SELECTS, INSERTS, UPDATES, WSDL responses, and so on for each deployed record. The level of detail is up to you—simple counts versus detailed descriptives—but it's essential to keep track, mostly for the sanity of you and your stakeholders who at some point will not be able to find a record that went AWOL during the source-to-target transmission. If said records are part of the error log, you should also include the record count and cause.

As much as possible, individual job runs should include the start date and time of the job as well as the finish date and time. In this manner, you will be able to track the "deltas" for future updates which not only help allocate the time you will need for later migration tests but also let you know when something is out of whack: a job that usually takes 5 minutes to execute but, for one cycle takes more than 30 minutes, is experiencing some problem along the route. Network analysis tools such as Wireshark[16] or traffic monitors such as Charles[17] will be an excellent place to begin your analysis.

Go-Live/Deployment Plan

The Go-Live/Deployment Plan occurs as the last step of the integration phase in which the integration team, now ready to proceed with an organized deployment, submits the step-by-step, start-to-finish plan to perform the migration, *including dependencies.* Creating this document should be relatively simple if you have followed the previous steps in this chapter—the Data Migration Process Flow Design document already contains sections marked "Order of Operations" and "Deployment" that serve this purpose. Of course, in that document, only the integration itself is described. In the Go-Live/Deployment Plan, the entire process from start to finish should be documented and not just those related to the migration portion (hence the emphasis above of "including dependencies").

The Go-Live/Deployment Plan is more of a communication tool than may be apparent at the outset. For the internal team, this deliverable requires an agreed-upon strategy of deployment order among each team member and, if properly aligned, will result in a smooth delivery process in which team members confidently will communicate each step to the others and subsequently provide signoff once complete or, if any unexpected issues occur, will enable them to revise or roll back.

For external teams, the Go-Live/Deployment Plan serves as a checklist of steps that the deployment team must take before they can call it a day. This activity allows stakeholders and business owners to know precisely what needs to take place, how

[16]"FREE Response Time Viewer for Wireshark | Solarwinds." 2019. *Solarwinds.com.* www.solarwinds.com/free-tools/response-time-viewer-for-wireshark

[17]"Charles Web Debugging Proxy • HTTP Monitor/HTTP Proxy/HTTPS & SSL Proxy/Reverse Proxy." 2019. *Charlesproxy.com.* www.charlesproxy.com/

long (on an estimated timeframe) Production will be shut down, and which team is responsible for the activity at hand. This resulting awareness has a much more calming effect than less organized deployments where the integration feature is assumed to be the "simple activity of button-pushing."

Post-deployment: Maintenance and Updates

Once the migration project is deployed to a Production environment, the obvious next step is to store the complete set of deliverables in an easy-to-find location, such as a shared corporate drive or content management system. While you may think that these documents can be filed away never to see the light of day, think again. Unless this is a one-time migration, your process will continue to grow and adapt along with the business needs, and you'll need to reference them, sometimes without warning. Three potential scenarios that come to mind are the following:

1. Data exceptions are the norm, and, at some point, the system will report an error, and someone at the target side is going to be highly agitated, highly confused, or both. You'll need first to figure out which field is failing and the details behind that transformation. The Source-to-Target mapping is the best starting point to begin your analysis, followed by the Migration Process Flow Design and ETL scripts.

2. Stakeholders may want to upgrade the existing integration process to include more fields or streamline the current code. Having these documents at hand will be a necessity when recalibrating your requirements.

3. You will want to audit any changes to systems that may seem unrelated to your process, but have an upstream impact, such as changed data in the source platform. Any time you hear of system enhancements that tangentially touch your inbound records, you'll want to go back to your documents and verify the impact. It's much easier to sound the alarm before the daily integration happens than to arrive on a Monday morning and find that your source table now holds string values instead of numbers and, consequently, your target table does too.

With this understanding, teams should recognize that these documents represent a snapshot of our integration process' current state and any changes performed on the source, ETL, or target platform due to bug fixes, patches, upgrades, or other modifications should be added to the appropriate documents. It's essential to maintain this upkeep—out-of-date information is sometimes worse than no information at all. And yet, like many of the other guidelines associated with project management, post-deployment teams ignore this critical step. Why? It's not always clear, but I can surmise two reasons:

1. Lack of Ownership: The staff who perform the O&M duties of a system post-deployment are often different than those who developed the product. Being in an O&M mode usually requires quick turnaround and resolution compared to a product team that assumes documentation as part of their responsibility. In other words, for the O&M team, rewriting these documents is just not a priority.

2. Lack of Understanding: The people who modify these deliverables may not understand the new requirements, may not know how to write them verbally, or—most likely—may have forgotten to update them at the appropriate time.

The integration team must address these risks at the outset, clearly acknowledging that documents must be updated consistently throughout the project lifetime and that it is the direct responsibility of the owners of the process (e.g., O&M) to store the latest versions the moment these changes deploy.

Summary

We've covered most of the integration phases in this chapter, starting from the project initiation and extending to go-live and beyond. At this point, you should recognize that documentation is not a "should" but a "must." It may seem counterintuitive, but the more effort to solidify the base requirements and mappings during the initial stages, the more flexibility the team has in shifting last-minute requests later down the line. This flexibility occurs because each document is closely related to the one preceding it. Modifying a set of requirements creates a ripple that starts at the initiation phase and flows through the definition, design, development, and implementation.

Because of these dependencies, we have the remarkable ability to trace each line of our transformation code back to our business requirements. If these requirements should fall out of alignment at the eleventh hour, then modifying the ETL code to sync back up with them is a relatively straightforward fix from the root document.

In the next chapter, we'll examine the fundamentals of that ETL code, describe the steps needed to build a simple service, and discuss the pros and cons of several popular ETL software applications.

CHAPTER 5

Choosing an ETL Tool

You must choose. But choose wisely...

—Grail Knight, *Indiana Jones and the Last Crusade* (1989)[1]

Introduction

In previous chapters, we have discussed not only the basics of migration/integration but also the types of documents required to develop a communication flow and strategic plan. The central theme through all this is that *detail matters*. And maintaining this level of detail is nowhere more critical than in the hub of your design known as the extraction, transformation, and loading (ETL) middleware. We covered the features of this component to some degree in Chapter 2 and the accompanying Source-to-Target mapping spreadsheet in Chapter 4. Because it has such a significant impact as to the success or failure of your project, this chapter will focus on the options available to you for choosing the right tools and discuss several of the ETL tools currently in the marketplace that will best fit your integration needs.

ETL Vs. ELT

Let me start by suggesting that you interpret the acronym ETL as literal. That is, you are performing straight **e**xtraction, **t**ransformation, and **l**oading operations. In Figure 5-1, you can see the "not-so-simple" diagram for the ETL and the corresponding components we discussed in Chapter 2.

---

[1]"Grail Knight: But Choose Wisely, for While the True Grail Will Bring You Life, the False Grail Will Take It from You." 2019. *Quotes.net.* www.quotes.net/mquote/46785

J. Goldfedder, *Building a Data Integration Team*, https://doi.org/10.1007/978-1-4842-5653-4_5

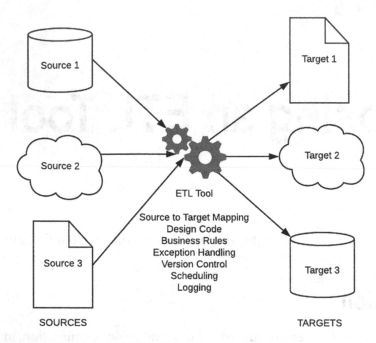

Figure 5-1. *The Not-So-Simple ETL Diagram Revisited*

ETL, in its pure form, indicates that we are pulling data from the source (extracting), performing some operation on the data to either change or manipulate its flow (transformation), and then pushing the latest version of this data into the target (loading).

It is also possible to reverse the transformation-load sequence so that you have a designation called extraction, loading, and transformation (ELT). In the ELT approach, after the data is extracted, the data source values are moved into a single, centralized data repository, which can be computed on the fly into analytic reporting systems (see Figure 5-2). In the old days (i.e., a decade ago), this would have been challenging due to processing and scalability issues, but with today's cloud-based infrastructure mixed with Big Data tools such as Hadoop, systems can support ample storage and scalable compute.[2]

---

[2]"ETL vs. ELT: The Difference Is in the How." 2019. *Blog.panoply.io*. https://blog.panoply.io/
etl-vs-elt-the-difference-is-in-the-how

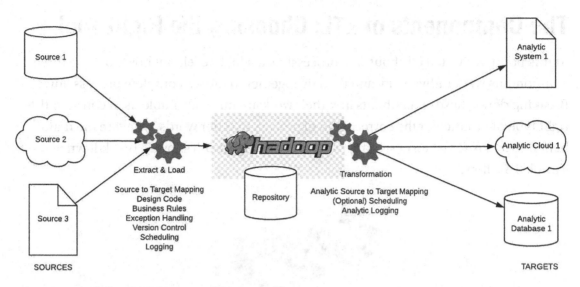

Figure 5-2. *The ELT Process (Proposed)*

The ELT process is still evolving but is referenced frequently enough in recent documents that it's worth mentioning. We won't be delving into this design for the remainder of this book, but I recommend that teams keep one eye open for technologies and skillsets that could incorporate this model. The promise of unlimited, on-demand access to entire datasets is tantalizing and one which many executives and BI personnel will want to explore further.

ETL As Middleware

It's important to note that while an ETL tool often exists separately from the source and target systems, it is not always the case. It is quite possible to have an ETL process that lives within the source system, such as a web service that propels data directly to an external endpoint, or within the target system, such as a shared process that pulls data from the source. Simple solutions are essential for these types of projects. Keep in mind, however, that although your system may have embedded hooks from the source to the target without the need for middleware, it is the *concept* of ETL with which we are concerned. Your solution will need to be something that can handle the ease of movement alongside the ease of transformation; and, in whatever way you want to design it, the ETL sequence will remain consistent.

The Components of ETL: Choosing the Right Tool

At this point, we've talked about ETL processing at a high level. But how do these three components work individually and then tie together to form a complete process flow? Breaking down these components into their workstreams will enable us to consider the right type of product for the correct kind of project. In other words, what are the main benefits to look for when designing your solution? Figure 5-3 shows a breakdown of the sample ETL flow.

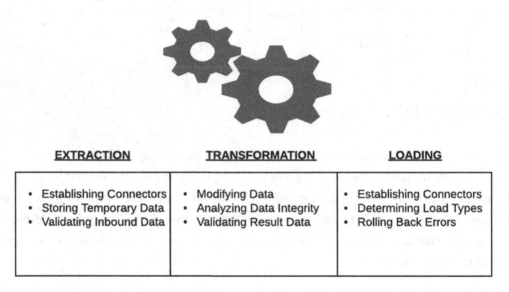

EXTRACTION	**TRANSFORMATION**	**LOADING**
• Establishing Connectors • Storing Temporary Data • Validating Inbound Data	• Modifying Data • Analyzing Data Integrity • Validating Result Data	• Establishing Connectors • Determining Load Types • Rolling Back Errors

Figure 5-3. *Breakdown of the ETL Process: Choosing the Right Tool*

Extraction

Our process starts when we first retrieve the data from our source system. Like all things integration related, there are a few concepts to consider when choosing the right ETL tool, including establishing connectors, storing temporary data, and validating inbound data.

Establishing Connectors

In the first stage, extraction, data is retrieved from the source systems—cloud, document, database—via a connector. A connector is a way to connect with the many disparate sources that exist in modern organizations.[3] Generally, a connector is a specialized translator that allows one system to read data housed in a proprietary system that usually is incompatible. As part of the translation, the connector must provide information specific to that proprietary system such as a JDBC/ODBC connection string, an endpoint, a port number, a database name, a username, a password, and so on; searching against online product documentation usually provides the requirements for writing a clean connection string. Vendors typically bundle proprietary connectors along with the commercial software, and many off-the-shelf ETL tools offer them as part of the complete package. Naturally, the more complex and disparate your data sources are, the more connectors you will want available.

Storing Temporary Data

Once the connection is established, the requested data is retrieved and is stored in what we call the temporary staging area.[4] On do-it-yourself types of migrations, this staging area could be any number of temporary processing repositories like database tables, CSV files, or spreadsheet files. In the case of most third-party ETL tools, it's a temporary buffer selected and maintained by the ETL tool itself.

Some concerns may arise during this step of the process as temporary data, often referred to as "data in transit",[5] may contain Personally Identifiable Information (PII) related to customers, accounts, or other secured information.[6] Of course, security is a concern across your enterprise, but this level of exposure is particularly susceptible during the extraction-storage process. To keep your data from prying eyes, make sure that the solution either (a) restricts the amount of sensitive data you are storing, (b) secures the data in motion using proper encryption techniques, or (c) houses the

---

[3]"ETL (Extract, Transform and Load)." 2019. *Syncsort.* www.syncsort.com/en/glossary/etl

[4]2019. *Guru99.com.* www.guru99.com/etl-extract-load-process.html

[5]"Data in Transit—An Overview | Sciencedirect Topics." 2019. *Sciencedirect.com.* www.sciencedirect.com/topics/computer-science/data-in-transit

[6]"What Is Personally Identifiable Information (PII)?" 2019. *Searchfinancialsecurity.* https://searchfinancialsecurity.techtarget.com/definition/personally-identifiable-information

temporary data behind a firewall on a secure system accessible by only your most trusted personnel. Be careful not to be too extreme, however, as locking down too much of your data can be just as troublesome as leaving it completely open. The chosen ETL solution should be able to help you find the right balance between too much and too little, so keep this in mind when researching the alternatives.

For some additional thoughts on this topic, refer to *https://www.helpnetsecurity. com/2016/10/25/securing-data-in-motion/*[7] and *https://pulse.microsoft.com/ en-ie/technology-lifestyle-en-ie/na/fa3-data-in-motion-how-to-protect-it-5- key-considerations/*.[8]

Validating Inbound Data

Throughout the extraction process, you'll want to make sure that you are pulling the right fields, making sure that you have a exact match between your source and stored data. This validation can and should happen throughout the ETL process, but it is essential for this first phase since data loss at this step will not be traced throughout the later stages. Some of the validation techniques you may want to test are ensuring that data types like strings and numbers are consistent, duplicated or fragmented data is removed, and primary keys for each of your objects are included. Remember, the final data output is only as good as the initial data input. If you are moving invalid data during your extraction, then remediation during subsequent steps is nothing short of a huge challenge.

Transformation

Unless you are dealing with a direct 1:1 map of your data where your source matches your target, you must manipulate your staged data to match the expected format of your target system. This activity is where the actual effectiveness of your chosen ETL tool comes into play. There are several factors to consider when making your transformation decisions, such as modifying data and validating the results.

[7]"Best Practices for Securing Your Data In-Motion—Help Net Security." 2019. *Help Net Security*. www.helpnetsecurity.com/2016/10/25/securing-data-in-motion/

[8]"Data in Motion—How to Protect It—5 Key Considerations." 2019. *Microsoft Pulse*. https://pulse.microsoft.com/en-ie/technology-lifestyle-en-ie/na/ fa3-data-in-motion-how-to-protect-it-5-key-considerations/

Modifying Data

The more complicated the transformation, the more internal functionality your ETL tool will need to have. Data that does not require manipulation is called *direct move* or *pass-through* data,[9] and we usually identify it as such on the Transformation Rules section of the Source-to-Target Mapping (see Chapter 4).

Transformation, at its most basic level, involves applying a set of functions on the extracted data. How these functions are coded and triggered is perhaps the most critical step in determining the best tool for your team. Some ETL products use Java for transformations (Talend), while others may inherit their codebase from Microsoft scripting (SSIS), JavaScript (Pentaho), or a choice of programming languages (Dell Boomi). It seldom helps teams hit the ground running when developers and support staff need to learn an entirely new language from scratch. Pairing the right transformation syntax with the skillset of your team will make a massive difference in your beginning productivity.

Analyzing Data Integrity

I mentioned earlier that the data provided by the source would be stored in a staging area. During the transformation phase, programmatic rules are applied, which results in a modified value. To determine the integrity of our transformation, we need to pose three questions:

1. Is my data accurate? For example, can the transformed value be traced back to the source?

2. Is my data complete? For example, are fields denoted as NOT NULL in the target system populated with a valid value?

3. Is my data consistent? For example, have we applied the same rules across the board for similar values?[10]

---

[9]2019. *Guru99.com.* www.guru99.com/etl-extract-load-process.html

[10]"What Is Data Integrity and Why Is It Important?—Talend." 2019. *Talend Real-Time Open Source Data Integration Software.* www.talend.com/resources/what-is-data-integrity/

All three questions matter, and failure to meet any of them will trip up the project somewhere along the way. We'll find it either during deployment when we get a dreaded "Cannot insert NULL into NOT NULL value"[11] or later down the line when our reporting system coyly identifies four separate accounts labeled "International Business Machines," "IBM," "IBM Corp.," and "I.B.M."

Of course, we want to avoid and patch any data integration errors that we find during our transformation process. Given that our projects literally might have millions of data points to cover, this is easier said than done. I would go so far as to say that lack of data integrity is probably the most significant cause of bugs following an initial data migration. What can we do to resolve the potential for these types of errors? Here are two suggestions I've tried:

1. Update at the source.

    We discussed in a previous chapter the concept of profiling—the process of reviewing source data to understand the structure, content, and interrelationships. During your profiling phase, pay special attention to specific patterns that account for most of the standard data integrity issues:

    - Different spellings of names/nicknames identified alongside email (Beth versus Elizabeth versus Liz, all with the same email address)

    - Different organization spellings (IBM, I.B.M., IBM Corp.)

    - NULL values in the source that require population in the target

    - Alphanumeric characters mixed with data that should be numbers only

    - Misspellings or inconsistencies to manually entered values such as addresses or products

---

[11]"Oracle/PLSQL: ORA-01400 Error Message." 2019. *Techonthenet.com*. www.techonthenet.com/ oracle/errors/ora01400.php

2. Analyze and update post-transformation.

    If, for whatever reason, you cannot correct (or identify) the data at the source, investigate and provide exception logic to your transformed data. This approach will require you to store the processed data in yet another temporary storage platform, but it will allow you to perform a makeshift profiling analysis that will show many more data integrity errors than could be found simply by eyeballing your load extract.

    Although you can do it, be wary when attempting to modify badly aligned data outside of the source system. While it may seem more straightforward to modify that over which you have control, the most significant deficiency with updating in your ETL or staging platform is that you are creating narrow rules that must be maintained. That is, an update to one system necessitates an update to another, creating a dependency you may not want.

    For example, imagine that you hardcode transformation logic that converts all variations of "IBM," "I.B.M.," "International Business Machines," and so on into a single value: "IBM Corporation." This is relatively easy to do under your team's control and it saves time upfront as you do not have to change data in the source system. Five months later, the team from the source system makes the seemingly innocuous decision to update the target value of "IBM Corporation" into "IBM Corp." If (and this is a big "if") they decide to tell your team, are you ready to scour your ETL code and find where you placed that hardcoded logic? Are you then prepared to test and maintain every production change that requires similar exception logic changes? Forever and ever? Although it sounds like an exaggeration, you can see how taking data integrity ownership outside of the source system can lead to some significant roadmap upheavals. I would recommend avoiding as many of these update scenarios as possible, unless it really is more advantageous in the here and now, such as with the one-off migration.

    This brings us to the third option, which is more of a default.

3. Do nothing.

   If requesting a source update does not work, and you think building exception logic is a bad idea, then let the data make its way into the target as is. Yes, it will lack data integrity, but it will be *there*. As long as you can trace it to the root cause (i.e., a particular source field), remediation can shift to the target system cleanup crew. What's most important is that you avoid any unnecessary surprises. Warn teams ahead of time what you face and give them the pros and cons of all options involved, even the default of doing nothing. Identify the decision in the Notes column of the STTM spreadsheet and provide a status report that can go up the chain in case last-minute decisions are made.

Validating Result Data

The key to any data transformation is ensuring that the physical change to the data will correctly load into the target. The aspect of validating result data runs the gamut of all the transformations we have to complete, including filtering columns, merging lookup values, converting measurements like time and dates to a standard format, and mapping inconsistencies to single units ("1" for Male, "2" for Female, "3" for Binary, and so on). The data validation step is more about confirming the manipulation of the data, rather than whether it matches the source through data integrity. Of course, both data validation and data integrity go hand in hand, and it can be tough to reconcile the two concepts. This example may help:

My team was involved with migrating an international email correspondence database. Some of the correspondence was written entirely in Greek characters, some in Russian, some in German, and some in English. The migration was a relatively simple one in which we would take the specific character set and move from the source system (a Postgres server) through an ETL platform (Pentaho) into the target (Salesforce). One of the first things we discovered was that try as we might, we could only get the Russian Cyrillic characters to show up as gibberish. Same for the Greek characters. But German and English seemed to work just fine. I should mention that we didn't receive any error messages during the load. In other words, everything processed, only not with the distinct international character sets of Greek and Russian.

We discovered during testing that the cause was through the character set we had chosen in our target; we were using an ASCII Latin character set when we should have chosen a character set that included international symbols such as UTF-8 (a great explanation on the use of ASCII versus other encoding sets is available at *https://stackoverflow.com/questions/2241348/what-is-unicode-utf-8-utf-16*).[12]

I give this example to illustrate how the data integrity worked as designed—our accuracy, completion, and consistency of our transformed data matched in terms of content (at least, as far as our literary assessment of Russian and Greek could be). What was off was our data validation due to transformation: we processed the wrong encoding feature, a function of the ETL tool itself. The resolution required us to both look at the data integrity (the data) and the data validation result (the transformation itself), make the correct assessment, and move forward by adjusting our default character set.

When you choose your ETL tool, you'll want to make sure you get a balance on both the data integrity and data validation steps. The most critical features you'll test will be the ability to quickly convert your staging data through functions via a familiar programming language, to automate searching the errors intrinsic in the transformed data, and then to remediate these errors in the smallest number of clickable or programmatic steps.

Loading

Loading is the last phase of the ETL process and generally the one most people relate to when we discuss the "push-button" approach to data migration. That is, push a button, and data moves from the source to the target with extracts full and transformations complete. We know that's not the default position we should take, but we still hold the acknowledgment that someday, at some point, our data will be close to that final point where we need to migrate our data, set up our nightly feeds, and get signoff. We're not too far off from this (and we'll discuss more about this button-pushing in Chapter 7), and I always promise my team that once we get over this hump, drinks are on me.

In actuality, the load process will always require a bit of final tweaking and planning before we are ready to call it a day. In this section, we'll discuss several of the features of the load that we should be aware of when choosing the right ETL tool, such as establishing connectors, determining load types, and rolling back errors.

---

[12]"What Is Unicode, UTF-8, UTF-16?" 2019. *Stack Overflow.* https://stackoverflow.com/questions/2241348/what-is-unicode-utf-8-utf-16

Establishing Connectors

We're returning to the topic of connectors one more time. We initially discussed building our extraction phase with our inbound connector, our proprietary data translator, firmly in mind. Now, we're going the opposite way so that instead of pulling data from the source (or opening a listener for a web service), we're inserting or updating data into the target. A big difference between the extraction and load connectors, however, is *time*. We may have multiple inbound transaction sources, but (in most cases) only a single outbound target and the data accumulates in our pipeline, making outbound loads much longer than retrieval.

As an example, let's say we have five source systems, each with 1 million records. Each one can be extracted, transformed, and profiled into our middleware server over five weeks. At the end of the five weeks, we're ready to conduct the one-night load of 5 million records into our target system. Thus, we had five weeks to move 5 million records but spent most of that time evaluating, rather than performing, the actual load. If our connector does not support bulk parallel loading (think Oracle SQL*Loader or SQL Server BCP), we're going to be running into trouble during our load phase as we are out of *time* (see Figure 5-4).

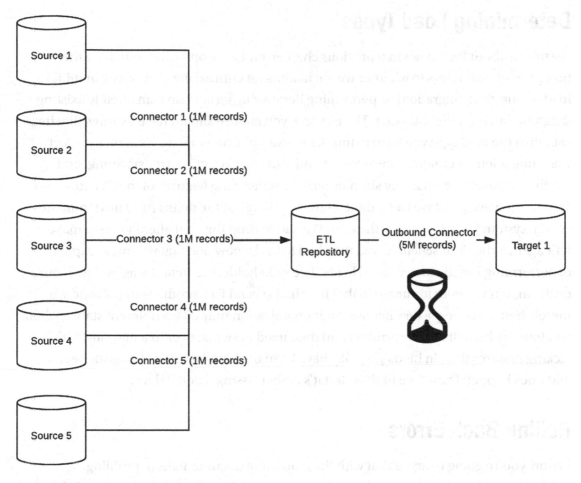

Figure 5-4. *Bulk Load into Target*

The key here is to know how much we need to load and what our ETL solution will support out of the box. If we don't have the time as part of the hourglass of Figure 5-4, we'll need to space out our loads to perhaps start at an earlier point in time than what we initially thought. There's nothing wrong with that approach, as long as the rest of the teams agrees with the impact that time plays in your load cycle. It's always better to start the phase early than run out of time due to false assumptions.

Determining Load Types

We talked about load types in a previous chapter, and we won't dwell much on them here. A load type refers to whether we are loading an entire dataset at once (an initial load or one-time migration) or performing iterative upserts against an already existing database (an incremental load). The ETL tool you choose should have features that help establish the load type you have in mind. For example, one tool we used on a project was quite adept at creating new one-time migrations, extracting, transforming, and loading the data in a relatively short order. The scheduling features of the ETL tool were lacking, however, and we had a difficult time picking out the deltas (updates) from the source system from one day to the next. We had to drop this tool after failing to make it fit against the right schedule and then had to find a new one that was more capable of performing nightly incremental loads. The stakeholders reluctantly agreed with our decision, but we were fortunate in that they had several ETL products in use, and we merely had to request a new license. Your organization may take a different stance when you tout the benefits of one product and then need to switch over to a new one if it's lacking features that, in hindsight, may have been obvious. Yes, that change of heart can and does happen from time to time, but it's embarrassing when it does.

Rolling Back Errors

I know you're going to argue that with the amount of documentation, profiling, validation, and testing, your loads are going to proceed just fine with no errors. I also know you know I write that with sarcasm.

Errors will happen, more than you'd like, but less than you'd think. And, because of the terrific work you've done with all that documentation, profiling, validation, and testing, you'll most likely know precisely when and why it happened. Nine times out of ten, it will be due to something mostly out of your control, like an errant record excluded from your testing environment or something more insidious like a network timeout error over which you quite honestly have no control. Of course, you will have the occasional random issues ("whoops, missed that in my exception logic") and, at that point, chalk it up to a simple mistake, roll back the load, install a fix, and redeploy.

The ETL tool you choose should possess some of the features related to rollback or at least those that will help you track your data errors such as a running count of successes and failures, log files representing times and timeouts, and some semblance of what records failed and why—most database insert errors consist of the data and cause of the issue. Although the ETL tool does not necessarily need to have features that clean the target and reset for a new deployment, providing the ability for teams to track and recover gracefully from errors in a timely fashion should be a consideration.

Tools on the Market

We've discussed the tenants for architecting our ETL process and making the right choice in tools. For the rest of the chapter, let's talk about several of the ETL tools on the market today and their capabilities, pros, and cons. Before we begin, however, let me go over a few caveats, lest I write an opinion that will leave others with hurt feelings, angry emails, and, most importantly, negative reviews of this book and attacks on my character (which, arguably, might be the same thing):

1. The tools I've chosen to list are based on my own experience and do not represent any affiliation with any of the respective vendors. I've used them for professional development and believe I am in a position to evaluate them. There are many, many ETL tools on the market (Gartner Research has a detailed summary of those both in the cloud and on premise, so if you're looking for some pure research guidelines, check out the latest by searching the term "Gartner magic quadrant for data integration tools"). To identify and repeat what Gartner has already put together, all would require more time, pages, and expertise than I could ever hope to communicate.

2. The purpose of this section is to empower you with a starting point on ETL tool discovery. Where possible, I have provided links to these companies' web sites so you can take the reins and continue the evaluations on your own. In other words, learn by doing, and if you find something unique, let me know, and I will incorporate your findings with my own.

3. This list is ever-changing, and what we know today will undoubtedly be different in five years. For me (and hopefully my editors), this represents a promise to write the next edition of this book sooner rather than never.

If we're ready then, let's start by discussing the first of our tools.

Jitterbit

Web site: www.jitterbit.com/

Review: Jitterbit was one of the first cloud-based ETL tools I used, and the experience was a positive one: using its freemium Salesforce Data Loader, I was able to build some excellent, scheduled integrations that took place in the cloud. Objects (the Salesforce equivalent of database tables) could be moved in hours, not days, using a sophisticated GUI (see Figure 5-5). We were clear we wanted to use this tool as our database backup system, and it served the need well. We were a bit stymied when the integrations became more complicated, but as time and technology have advanced, Jitterbit is offering more capabilities for API auto-creation and API management, and its future looks promising for its base of small and midsize companies. If you're just starting with ETL and the design is not too complicated, definitely explore the trial for this, as the company offers both on-premise and cloud-based solutions.

Pros: Simple to configure and deploy with relatively little downtime. Can handle a multitude of data connectors, including SAS, Salesforce, database, and web services. Technical support is very helpful and willing to answer most questions.

Cons: As integrations become more complex, so does the setup. Documentation at the time was sparse, and we did have multiple questions about security for cloud-based offerings.

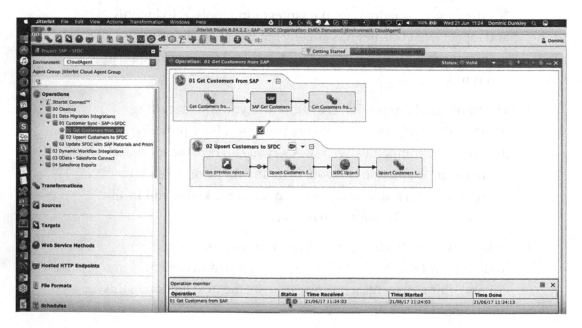

Figure 5-5. *Jitterbit API Transformation*

Talend

Web site: www.talend.com

Review: The Talend ecosystem represents a suite of tools, including Talend Open Studio, Talend Data Management Platform, Talend Data Services Platform, and Talend Integration Cloud. Its complete data management and integration portfolio is part of Talend Data Fabric, which includes data integration, data preparation, data catalog, data stewardship, and API management capabilities. With all these capabilities, Talend can perform against the most complex of ETL scenarios. Best of all, Talend maintains an open source community, so many of its tools in its Open Studio subscription are free to use (see Figure 5-6).[13] Personally, I love the idea of a complex product at no cost. However, Talend supports a Java Code Generator, which makes use of open source Java libraries. If you're not a Java developer, the learning curve might be extreme.

Pros: Great set of tools maintained by an open source community. Supports most, if not all, of the advanced ETL solutions you'll need. A great solution is you have a development team with Java skills.

Cons: If you're not already a Java aficionado, learning Talend can be an uphill battle. If the direction of your organization is one for extreme software development, this may be the tool for you. Otherwise, you may have difficulty finding team members to support your integration if and when you need to patch operations.

---

[13]"Talend Downloads: ETL Tools, Data Integration, and More." 2019. *Talend Real-Time Open Source Data Integration Software*. www.talend.com/download/

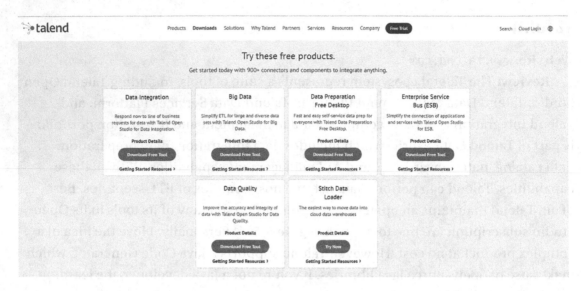

Figure 5-6. *Talend Open Studio Free Products*

Dell Boomi

Web site: `https://boomi.com/`

Review: Dell Boomi is one of those tools that I've used time and time again, and always seem to migrate toward (pun intended). If I need a high-end ETL processing solution with scheduling capabilities, I will mention Boomi to my clients, noting its ease of use for drag-and-drop GUI functionality (see Figure 5-7), no-nonsense approach to documentation, community contributions, and ability to run its agent, known as an Atom, truly remote, either behind a firewall for adding security or in the cloud. Boomi design does take a bit of getting used to, especially when it comes to persisting properties throughout an integration, but once you have this understanding in place, it's relatively easy to test, deploy, and maintain version control. The biggest negative for me is the pricing model, which seems to charge one license for each connector you own for each URL. That is, if you want to connect to one database with a specific endpoint, then you pay the retail rate for one connector. If you then want to connect to the same database, but then across a different endpoint, you pay for a separate license. There are workarounds for this, but it seems like an initial high up-front cost. If your ETL design doesn't require the high intensity that Boomi provides, this tool may not be right for your organization.

Pros: Easy to set up, deploy, and commit versioning control once you take the appropriate (online!) courses. Everything is spelled out for you with the use of tutorials, telephone support, and community forums. Because it is cloud based, there is little maintenance of the application, and built-in API calls allow you to perform some genuinely automated DevOps transactions (we'll discuss DevOps in Chapter 7).

Cons: A hefty price tag if you are trying to get advanced features like single sign-on, multiple connectors to same-source products, and unlimited customer service. Also, some aspects of Boomi that might be considered easier in other tools, like modifying data, may not be built-in and require the creation of customized scripts in either Groovy or JavaScript. Make sure you have developers with the right skillsets and a bit of patience, and you can make it work for you.

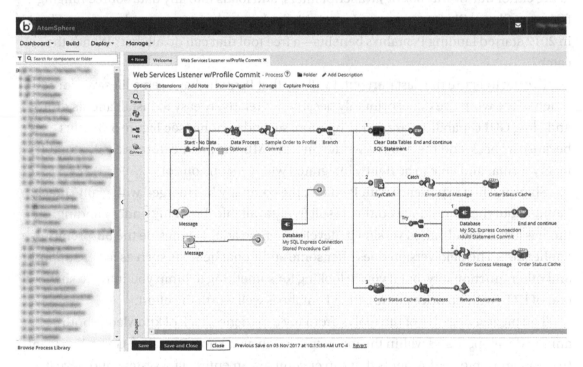

Figure 5-7. *Dell Boomi Process Window*

Pentaho Data Integration (PDI)

Web site: https://community.hitachivantara.com/s/article/data-integration-kettle (Community)

www.hitachivantara.com/en-us/products/data-management-analytics/pentaho-platform/pentaho-data-integration.html (Enterprise)

Review: Pentaho Data Integration was founded in the early 2000s with the design purely open source. This openness meant that the system would have free, readable metadata (XML) standards and open API standards, be easy to set up (2 minutes, give or take), support all kinds of databases, and allow data conversion to/from any format.[14] The result was a free product that consumes virtually any data format, transforms it using either out-of-the-box or JavaScript filters, and loads into any data source ranging from text files to Big Data systems. I was initially skeptical when a coworker of mine back in 2012 started lauding Pentaho's benefits—a free tool that can do all that? What's the catch?

I've yet to figure that last part out. I will say that Pentaho has been a lifesaver for much of the work I've done, primarily because it's relatively easy to install and its drop-and-drag GUI capabilities are, in my opinion, second to none (see Figure 5-8). Plus, because its back-end metadata is written in text XML, the architecture is easily storable in any format and able to be tightly integrated with version control.

Since my first experience with Pentaho, the company has merged with giant Hitachi Vantara, but the community edition is still freely available. From my understanding, there is also a cloud-based version in development to adapt alongside the on-premise application. The paid version does offer some additional benefits such as faster support and other functionality, but if you're looking for something to jump you into the shallow end of ETL (with no price point!), then Pentaho is well worth the effort.

The biggest negative of the tool is, from my experience, lack of knowledge both among developers and within the marketplace. Oh, you know Pentaho? Great. You want to create multiple deployments that can encompass an entire data system and have it ready to run in a few weeks? No problem. Do you want to find other people who can help support the tool after you leave? That's going to be an issue. But if you're willing to change your shop to make Pentaho the de facto tool, I think you could probably get a lot of mileage out of it.

---

[14]Matt Casters, Roland Bouman, and Jos van Dongen. 2010. *Pentaho Kettle Solutions.* Indianapolis: Wiley.

Pros: Because it was my first significant encounter with an easy-to-use ETL tool, I speak rather highly of it. As I always tell people, "PDI lets me do somersaults with my data." You may not feel the same, however, and I cannot necessarily speak as to how the tool has fared under the recent Hitachi Vantara acquisition. Still, if you feel adventurous and want to give it a try, I would recommend it. The community edition is free, so you literally have nothing to lose.

Cons: PDI tends to be a tool overshadowed in the marketplace by some of the more prominent names, and therefore finding staff who understand the design and are willing to support this tool can be a problem. For one-off migrations, PDI works very well. For incremental loads (i.e., nightly integrations), PDI has some features that are lacking, such as graceful error handling.

We'll return to more Pentaho in the next chapter when we build our sample ETL process.

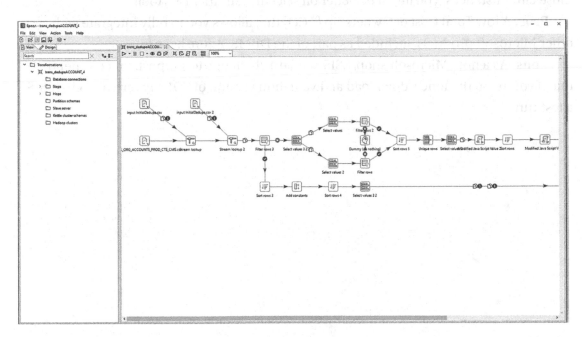

Figure 5-8. *Pentaho Data Integration Main Window*

Microsoft SQL Server Integration Services (SSIS)

Web site: https://docs.microsoft.com/en-us/sql/integration-services/sql-server-integration-services?redirectedfrom=MSDN&view=sql-server-ver15

Review: It was in the age of dinosaurs (2003) when I was first introduced to the first iteration of SSIS, known as Data Transformation Services (DTS), to replicate an Oracle database into a Microsoft SQL Server reporting warehouse. Since that time, SSIS has come a long way and is embedded in Microsoft products both on premise via the SQL Server DBMS license and in the cloud via the Azure Data Factory cloud data integration service. In other words, when you use Microsoft as your base, SSIS is pretty much the standard. From all accounts, SSIS is quick to implement, is easy to use, and integrates fully with other Microsoft SQL/Azure products (see Figure 5-9). The main issue arises when you are not a Microsoft shop and have no plans to purchase or use the main product lines. Under those circumstances, you might be better off selecting another ETL tool.

Pros: A low Total Cost of Ownership (TCO) that allows you to fully integrate with other Microsoft products, included as part of the DBMS/Azure license.

Cons: As a non-Microsoft shop, SSIS can be a challenge to support. I recommend that if you're on the fence, download an Evaluation version of SQL Server[15] and give SSIS a test run.

---

[15]"Microsoft Evaluation Center." 2019. *Microsoft.com*. www.microsoft.com/en-us/evalcenter/evaluate-sql-server

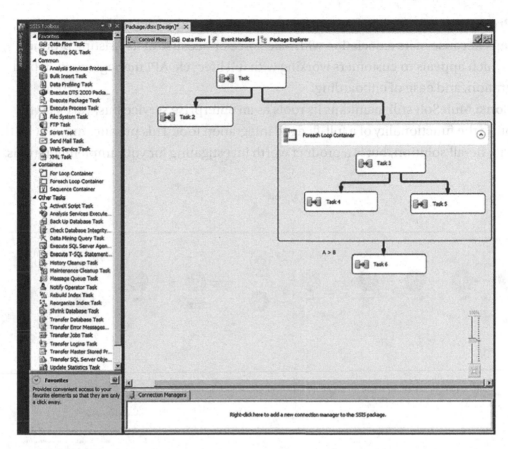

Figure 5-9. *SSIS Control Flow*

MuleSoft

Web site: www.mulesoft.com/

Review: MuleSoft was founded in 2006 and became a Salesforce company through acquisition in May 2018. Initially, MuleSoft provided enterprise service bus (ESB) open source software and, in 2013, became one of the first pure integration vendors in the cloud after releasing its API management tool, Anypoint Platform (see Figure 5-10). My relationship with MuleSoft is limited, but I've heard through various channels that it is an excellent ETL tool with plugs-in to most environments. According to Gartner reports, MuleSoft has doubled its client base in the last several years and provides strong API management, security support, multi-cloud deployment, and an open-core ESB. As with other tools that feature these advanced capabilities, your developers will need to have a more significant deal of technical know-how than with other products. Fortunately, MuleSoft has some excellent training, both online and in the classroom.

Pros: Currently, MuleSoft appears to be taking a healthy lead in the marketplace, perhaps because of its association with Salesforce or because of its existing product line, which appeals to customers working with full lifecycle API management, hybrid integration, and ease of onboarding.

Cons: MuleSoft still maintains its roots as an enterprise service bus, very slowly adopting the functionality of a full-fledged integration tool. This product may not be the end-all, be-all solution, but is a product worth investigating for your implementations.

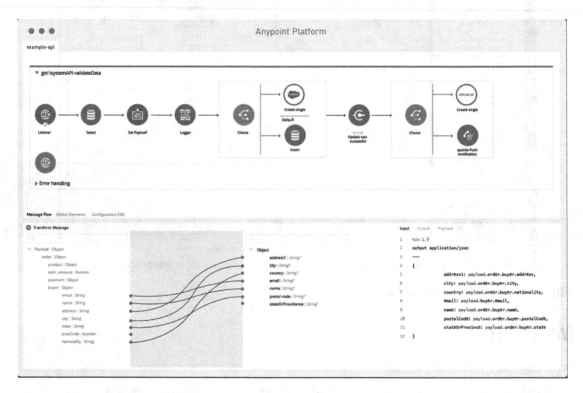

Figure 5-10. *MuleSoft Anypoint Platform*

Informatica

Web site: www.informatica.com

Review: No discussion of ETL would be complete without discussing Informatica, the first name associated with data management. The company has been around since 1993 and has gone through multiple iterations both on premise and then into the cloud, which it pioneered in 2007. I was certified as an Informatica Cloud Specialist in 2016, and since then, the company has evolved into the next generation known as Informatica Intelligent Cloud Services (IICS; see Figure 5-11).

I have a love-hate relationship with this product. It does the job expected by an integration team, and it does it *very well, s*o well that it probably should be on everyone's shortlist of tools. But it is also run by an institution that has its roots in data management, and I found that the existing technology sometimes lags compared to other vendors, although this may be changing with the latest cloud implementation. For me, the biggest challenge has been learning the tool. It is so feature-rich that for new users to embrace it fully requires training, long-term strategic planning, and full commitment.

Pros: Large market share. Generally considered the powerhouse player in the ETL space, which supports all aspects of migrations/integrations such as a broad set of connectors, security, metadata management, disaster recovery, manageability, standards compliance, and online technical support.

Cons: As with many advanced tools, Informatica has so many features, yet we have so little time to learn them all. As stated, the product is perhaps too much for some organizations. I have talked with developers who admit that using Informatica on smaller datasets is like "hitting a butterfly with a hammer." If your organization is serious about their data integration approach, then I would say to throw your team all in and do the research. Otherwise, consider the less robust tools I have mentioned.

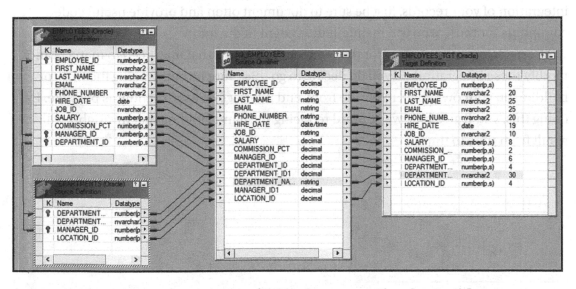

Figure 5-11. *Informatica Mapping (Taken from* www.edureka.co/blog/
informatica-etl/)

Scripting Languages

Web site: Various

Review: The last ETL tool on our list is not a third-party vendor product and further illustrates the point that ETL can come in all shapes and sizes. I've worked in startups and software firms who are technical enough that they do not need the typical drag-and-drop functionality offered by an SSIS or Informatica-like application, instead choosing to "roll their own" ETL through a programming language or pre-built libraries stored in Python and Perl (see Figure 5-12).[16] I think this is a legitimate approach: it removes the dependency on applications that can often bog down a project with the learning curve and financial costs. On the other hand, this type of implementation does require your teams to possess the breadth and knowledge to oversee maintenance and be able to swoop in quickly should any errors arise.

Several debates are available as to whether scripts are superior to vendor products (compare *https://tombreur.wordpress.com/2017/02/19/etl-is-dying/*[17] with *https://www.linkedin.com/pulse/etl-its-dead-yet-jarrett-goldfedder*[18]). Stick with whatever makes you feel comfortable.

Pros: For those with the bandwidth, scripting is a fair way to start the migration/integration of your records. Just be sure to document often and provide useful code comments for those who will maintain the system in the future.

Cons: Not a good strategy for the nontechnical teams that may need to manage and modify these integrations. If you do decide to go this route by outsourcing the work or building on your own, then make the front-end interface as user-friendly as possible. By doing this, you'll go a long way toward reducing the hand-holding that invariably will result from time to time.

---

[16]"Top Python ETL Tools (aka Airflow vs. the World)." 2019. *Blog.panoply.io.* https://blog. panoply.io/top-9-python-etl-tools-and-when-to-use-them

[17]"ETL Is Dying." 2019. *Data, Analytics and Beyond.* https://tombreur.wordpress. com/2017/02/19/etl-is-dying/

[18]Goldfedder, Jarrett. 2017. "ETL: It's Not Dead Yet." *Linkedin.com.* www.linkedin.com/pulse/ etl-its-dead-yet-jarrett-goldfedder

```python
import bonobo

def guess_email(**row):
    return {
        **row,
        'email': row['name'] + '@' + row['domain']
    }

graph = bonobo.Graph(
    bonobo.CsvReader('employees.csv'),
    bonobo.Filter(
        lambda **row: row['position'] != 'CEO'
    ),
    guess_email,
    bonobo.CsvWriter('employees.output.csv'),
)
```

Figure 5-12. Bonobo Sample (`www.bonobo-project.org/`)

Summary

In this chapter, we've covered the primary phases of the ETL process that will help you evaluate the right tool and then reviewed several of the applications to get you started. As I've noted, this is not a complete list, nor does it approach selection from a non-biased point of view. Yes, I have my preferences, and I'm willing to share them with whoever will listen. After devoting enough time and effort to the build process, I have learned what I need to complete a migration assignment as well as the red flags that warn me to stay away. The problem that results from this thinking, however, is that too much reliance on one product can close you from considering other tools that might provide substantial value. Due to some preconceived notions, we take the "safe" route—choosing the tool that may not be optimal, but that has always worked in the past—and risk losing out over the long run.

To avoid paralysis-by-analysis pitfalls in choosing your ETL tool, keep in mind that there are a lot of quality tools out there just as there are some not-so-good ones. I recommend you strongly consider your project requirements, think about the "perfect" tool you would need to get the job done, and then research the products that match as closely as possible to that level of perfection. Most likely, you won't find your Holy Grail. But, as the Grail Knight from the *Indiana Jones* movie cautioned, you will at least be in a better position to "choose wisely."

CHAPTER 6

A Sample ETL Project

There is no better insurance than the knowledge of how to do something the right way. There is no greater peace of mind than knowing you did it the right way.

—Jerry G. West[1]

Introduction

At this point, your team is in place, you have your documentation ready for writing, and you've picked out an ETL tool. We still have a few nitty-gritty details to hammer out, but before we dive deeper, I'd like to take this chapter to build a prototype. Because this is not a book on building a team and not a specific ETL solution, we'll walk through the steps one at a time, focusing more on the process rather than the technology.

For this design, we'll introduce you to the overall process using the community edition of Pentaho Data Integration (PDI), an on-premise application that you can download for free from Hitachi Vantara's web site. Of course, you can use whatever tool you would like, but keeping things comprehensive yet straightforward is the goal.

---

[1]"Do It Yourself Quotes (23 Quotes)." 2019. *Goodreads.com.* www.goodreads.com/quotes/tag/do-it-yourself

J. Goldfedder, *Building a Data Integration Team,* https://doi.org/10.1007/978-1-4842-5653-4_6

Project Management Phases Revisited

To start, let's review the project management phases that we covered in Chapter 4:

- Initiation

- Definition

- Design

- Development and implementation

- Maintenance

Initiation

The initiation phase is the birth of the idea—a project we want where we first vet our problem statement and consider its feasibility. It's where we build the proposal for a solution, choose our budget, and establish our teams.

Imagine that we work for the IT department of InfoMotors, a car dealership that tracks customer purchases in a text editor. These files are stored customer data (name, email), the car they bought (make, model, color, year), the price they paid, and the date purchased. Because InfoMotors is a new dealer, they do all their bookkeeping and reporting in Excel.

But things are changing, and in order to improve their efficiency and minimize data issues, management would like to migrate their text files into a new on-premise database. They are evaluating different teams that can handle the work and would want to determine a pricing structure and timeline. You are, of course, included in this discussion to ensure the assumptions are accurate and the plan is realistic.

Does this sound like something we can do? If so, then let's get started.

Definition

You have a clear understanding of what's expected with the minimal requirements of the plan. Your first step is to take this knowledge and iteratively populate the Data Migration Plan which, as we discussed in Chapter 4, serves as communication for the project background and purpose, the proposed migration and integration approach, any assumptions, constraints, risks, and the planned current and future state architecture.

At this point, we haven't established the technology, and the only things we know are that

1. We have customer data stored in comma-delimited and tab-delimited files.

2. We'll be migrating this data to the new SQLite database.

Note   I know many people who would compare the time required to document our design on multiple approaches and ask, "Why not just export the files DIRECTLY into the database one at a time? After all, surely that involves much less effort and less documentation and achieves the same purpose." You're right. In this case, it would. This exercise is a simple scenario, and the ones you'll be facing in real life will be much more complex. Even with this in mind, unless you know your data, you can't assume that all your documents will be consistent. In any case, the Data Migration Plan is where you build your case for the type of migration you've chosen through any of the various techniques like direct import, ETL scripts, or copy/paste from Excel spreadsheets.

We should have enough information to start populating the Data Migration template with our general understanding. For example:

Project Background and Purpose

- InfoMotors, a car dealership that stores customer data, has been storing customer information in text files and archiving the dataset at the end of the year.

- In order to improve their efficiency and minimize data issues, management would like to migrate their text files into a new on-premise database. The purpose of this plan is to elaborate on the design that will enable this data to move from source to target systems with transformations that meet the target system format specifications.

Proposed Migration and Integration Approach

- Using an ETL tool, we will be extracting data from two text files, performing transformations on the internal data to fit the target structure, and loading to the target database. Once migration is complete, future data will be entered directly on the target system.

Not a bad start, right? It's short and straightforward and communicates everything you know so far.

The positive to this approach is without even starting a single line of code, you've already explained your expectations and put the ball back into management's court. Imagine that during the Data Migration Document review, they get stuck on this line "Once migration is complete, future data will be entered directly on the target system."

"Wait," they say. "We talked it over and want to continue using our tab-delimited format at least until we train our staff. Can you move the latest data every two weeks?"

"Ah-ha," you say, and with a mighty stroke of the stylus, you've changed the requirement from "Once migration is complete, future data will be entered directly on the target system" to "Integration from a tab-delimited file will occur at the end of **every two weeks.**"

The Data Migration Plan is your roadmap from start to finish and is highly malleable. Just keep in mind that it's easier to change the blueprints of the house before building rather than after you've already laid the foundation and drywall.

Eventually, everyone will agree on the migration approach that you should use based on the evaluations discussed in Chapter 5 (as a refresher, review our security concerns, level of mapping complexity, and amount of custom coding). Of course, you'll need to match the approach to developer expertise. You'll often find that easier is sometimes better, but the quality will suffer in the process.

Based on our requirements, staff training, and implementation speed, we've evaluated our choices, have considered our long-term objectives, and (not surprisingly since this exercise is rigged) have decided to go with Pentaho Data Integration as our ETL tool.

Continuing with our Data Migration Plan, we can diagram our current and future state models to resemble Figures 6-1 and 6-2.

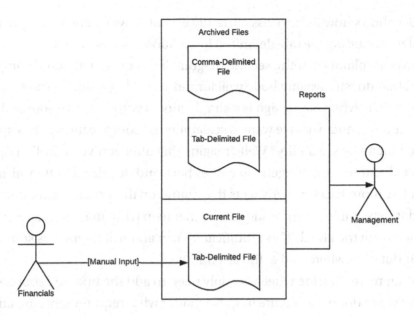

Figure 6-1. *Current State Model*

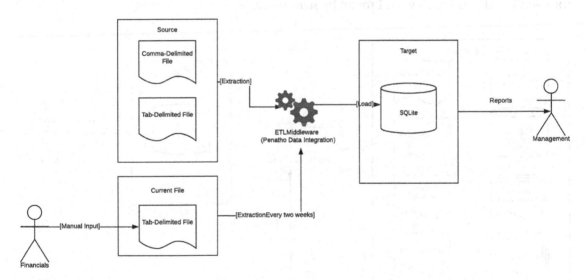

Figure 6-2. *Future State Model*

Figure 6-1 shows how the process currently executes, while Figure 6-2 presents the proposed plan, including the tab-delimited integration just discussed.

I've heard complaints that the second diagram looks overengineered compared to the first, and that doesn't usually bode well for those seeking a simple solution. That's accurate, especially when our design is a simple model with only two source documents. But systems change, and what we want is scalability, so complexity is to be expected.

What do I mean by scalability? Well, imagine that after you've identified the creation of two source documents, management comes back and decides that they also want to include a few more Excel spreadsheets they found on their sales teams' computers, additional database tables from headquarters that help with financials, and external records pulled from the cloud. This modification can and will happen as source systems often appear out of nowhere and at the last minute.

Rather than recreating the wheel, we only need to add the updated sources to the diagram, and we're done (see Figure 6-3). No matter what requirements are added, it can be expressed 99% of the time in a single diagram that requires just a bit of modification for each iteration. That's what I mean by *scalability*.

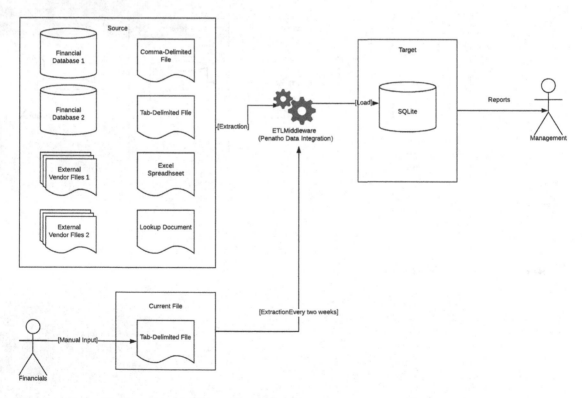

Figure 6-3. *Future State (More Complex)*

Design

We've specified our plan, come up with an approach, and have worked through the details with our stakeholders. Finally, we're able to start exploring our data and coding our solution. We'll produce several documents during this phase, each one building on the next. To begin with, we need to dive into the source data we've decided to tackle, to understand its structure, patterns, and discrepancies. This activity leads us to our next step, data profiling.

Data Profiling

For various reasons such as security concerns or storage limitations, we won't always have the full set of production data at our fingertips, and we'll have to make do with what we get. Even having a small sample of, say, 10% would be enough to get us started, but we will need something with which to work.

For our prototype, we have the two archived files available and can process them through the data profiling tool of our choice (see Chapter 4 for details). To save time, we'll glance at the first ten records in each file (see Figure 6-4).

```
id,first_name,last_name,email,car_make,car_model,car_color,car_year,price,date_purchased
1,Gabi,McMoyer,gmcmoyer0@joomla.org,Suzuki,Equator,Turquoise,2011,54498,2017-09-05
2,Harlie,Sodor,hsodor1@abc.net.au,Cadillac,STS,Mauv,2007,43328,2017-10-08
3,Cherianne,Wisdish,cwisdish2@rakuten.co.jp,Ford,Taurus,Pink,1989,26898,2017-02-27
4,Duky,Pollastrino,dpollastrino3@comsenz.com,Toyota,Land Cruiser,Maroon,1998,37297,2017-11-09
5,Reginauld,Hindshaw,rhindshaw4@squarespace.com,Buick,Verano,Green,2012,21264,2017-02-01
6,Xaviera,Skippon,xskippon5@wp.com,Mazda,MX-6,Blue,1997,45694,2017-09-04
7,Willa,Teese,wteese6@unesco.org,Pontiac,LeMans,Pink,1992,46824,2017-12-17
8,Grantley,Ilewicz,gilewicz7@ted.com,Dodge,Spirit,Orange,1995,20143,2017-07-08
9,Kristi,Downham,kdownham8@theglobeandmail.com,Spyker,C8 Double 12 S,Goldenrod,2006,29035,2017-05-07
10,Leighton,Tuley,ltuley9@si.edu,Mazda,626,Yellow,2001,27267,2017-10-22
```

```
id  first_name  last_name   email         car_make     car_model    car_color    car_year   price   date_purchased
1   Kaile       Southern    ksouthern0@spiegel.de    BMW M    Orange   2000    37869   05/02/2018
2   Koralle     Le Clercq   kleclercq1@ebay.co.uk    Chrysler  LHS Orange  2001    33389   02/03/2018
3   Gussi       Werlock     gwerlock2@ebay.co.uk     Pontiac LeMans  Fuscia  1967    59463   01/11/2018
4   Ruggiero    Sayles      rsayles3@examiner.com    Ford     Club Wagon  Green   1992    42554   10/10/2018
5   Beatrisa    Howselee    bhowselee4@illinois.edu Porsche Cayman  Khaki   2012    48139   06/24/2018
6   Matty       Desantis    mdesantis5@de.vu     Volkswagen Routan  Blue    2010    28861   05/08/2018
7   Marcus      Speechly    mspeechly6@wordpress.org   Infiniti   FX Maroon 2010    35746   05/03/2018
8   Kerry       Eytel       keytel7@infoseek.co.jp   Scion    tC Maroon 2008    28862   12/10/2018
9   Lilias      Tilmouth    ltilmouth8@delicious.com BMW Z4 M Roadster  Mauv    2009    30642   04/13/2018
10  Kinnie      Howgego     khowgego9@unicef.org     Infiniti   G25 Crimson 2012    42583   02/17/2018
```

Figure 6-4. *2017 CSV and 2018 TSV Sample Records*

A cursory review shows you that not only do files contain different delimiters (comma versus tab) but the date_purchased field appears to have a different format as well, representing YEAR-MONTH-DAY in the first file and MONTH/DAY/YEAR in the second.

Note   Returning to our previous discussion, it should be apparent why doing a direct import from the source files into the target SQLite database may not work the way you would expect. If you are not paying attention to the different delimiters and the different formats and adjusting your import controls for each, then you'll most likely corrupt your database and end up creating more work in the long run.

Even with this limited view, we have some options available. Referencing the Issues Log document, we can identify these findings down and then reach back to the data team and ask them to resend these files with synchronous formats (both comma delimited with standard date formats). We would highlight other questions in the Issues Log as well, such as why do some of these email addresses have international domains (answer: I randomly generated this list from *https://mockaroo.com*) or whether we should enforce constraints on exhaustive values like car model and car color. For example, do we allow typographical errors to be migrated into our new system if they exist in the source?

If we have the right ETL tool and the skilled workforce to do it, we should plan to transform our data in one fell swoop. This approach is the one we will want to take in this example, and we'll use that as our assumption moving forward.

Source-to-Target Mapping

Our Source-to-Target Mapping shows each inbound source field and how they will map to our target object. As discussed in Chapter 4, at a minimum, you will need to populate several columns related to the following:

- The name of the source system, file, table, and field

- The name of the target system, file, table, and field

- The rules behind the source-to-target transformation

Up to now, we haven't started a single line of code and are still just exploring our data. Now we need to bring in our data owners for the source and target systems and work with them to negotiate the details of which items populate where. The data owners do not necessarily need to be technical in understanding the conversions—that's on the integration side of the house—but they should be able to answer the straightforward questions of how the old data will map to the new.

Significant gaps will be identified and remediated during this step. We know we're dealing with at least two files for the initial load, a CSV and a TSV (tab-separated value), and we're migrating results into an SQLite database. What are the details we now need to know? For example, what's the name of the target database schema? Is it one table or multiple? What are the target field names, and do they correspond to our source field names? All these topics will get resolved throughout the discussion so that we can properly break down the mappings into a coherent document.

In many cases, the target data owners may not have an answer for you or will change their minds later in the project. Like the Data Migration Plan, changes are welcome at any point just as long as you communicate them through your documentation and have the bandwidth to perform your testing in a relatively short time. In Chapter 7, we'll talk about automating your tests to speed up your releases.

After questioning your source and target data owners—no more than the three of you, please!—you're able to document the first Source-to-Target Mapping spreadsheet. We'll post the bare-bones version in Table 6-1, although there is much more metadata that you could gather (see Chapter 4 for recommendations).

Table 6-1. Source-to-Target Mapping

Source System	Source Object	Source Field	Target System	Target Object	Target Field	Transformation Rule
File	Contacts_year1.csv	id	SQLITE	BUYER	EXTERNALID	'Contacts_year1' + Id
File	Contacts_year1.csv	first_name	SQLITE	BUYER	FIRST_NAME	Direct Transformation
File	Contacts_year1.csv	last_name	SQLITE	BUYER	LAST_NAME	Direct Transformation
File	Contacts_year1.csv	email	SQLITE	BUYER	EMAIL	Direct Transformation
File	Contacts_year1.csv	car_make	SQLITE	BUYER	CAR_MAKE	Direct Transformation
File	Contacts_year1.csv	car_model	SQLITE	BUYER	CAR_MODEL	Direct Transformation
File	Contacts_year1.csv	car_color	SQLITE	BUYER	CAR_COLOR	Direct Transformation
File	Contacts_year1.csv	car_year	SQLITE	BUYER	CAR_YEAR	Direct Transformation
File	Contacts_year1.csv	price	SQLITE	BUYER	PRICE	Direct Transformation
File	Contacts_year1.csv	date_purchased	SQLITE	BUYER	DATE_PURCHASED	Direct transformation with format YYYY-MM-DD
File	Contacts_year2.tsv	id	SQLITE	BUYER	EXTERNALID	'Contacts_year2' + Id
File	Contacts_year2.tsv	first_name	SQLITE	BUYER	FIRST_NAME	Direct Transformation
File	Contacts_year2.tsv	last_name	SQLITE	BUYER	LAST_NAME	Direct Transformation

(continued)

File	Contacts_year2.tsv	email	SQLITE	BUYER	EMAIL	Direct Transformation
File	Contacts_year2.tsv	car_make	SQLITE	BUYER	CAR_MAKE	Direct Transformation
File	Contacts_year2.tsv	car_model	SQLITE	BUYER	CAR_MODEL	Direct Transformation
File	Contacts_year2.tsv	car_color	SQLITE	BUYER	CAR_COLOR	Direct Transformation
File	Contacts_year2.tsv	car_year	SQLITE	BUYER	CAR_YEAR	Direct Transformation
File	Contacts_year2.tsv	price	SQLITE	BUYER	PRICE	Direct Transformation
File	Contacts_year2.tsv	date_purchased	SQLITE	BUYER	DATE_PURCHASED	Transform format to YYYY-MM-DD

Table 6-1 appears to cover a lot of information and might be overwhelming for some. But if you backtrack across it, you'll see that what you have are just the names of the source fields mapping to the same target fields, twice to represent the CSV and the TSV file. You'll also notice that we do not refer to any column as SourceTable or TargetTable. Instead, we are citing the "SourceObject" and "TargetObject." In that way, we can have any representation we need to reference, such as Excel spreadsheets, databases, and record files. Finally, you'll notice that our Transformation Rule calls out the expected flow that we code to map the extracted data against the target field. For example, our *date_purchased* field keeps the YYYY-MM-DD format from the first file but modifies the MM/DD/YYYY format to YYYY-MM-DD for the second file.

If you're not crazy about mapping row for row and you think maintainability of each column will be difficult—if a row in the target is added or modified, you'd have to scour the entire STTM—consider joining your source values with comma delimiters. It makes comprehension of individual fields more challenging when reviewing, but this join approach does clarify the overall mapping as a unit (see Table 6-2 for our concatenated STTM).

Table 6-2. Source-to-Target Mapping (Concatenated Source)

Source System	Source Object	Source Field	Target System	Target Object	Target Field	Transformation Rule
File, File	Contacts_year1.csv, Contacts_year2.tsv	id, id	SQLITE	BUYER	EXTERNALID	'Contacts_year1' + Id, 'Contacts_year2' + Id
File, File	Contacts_year1.csv, Contacts_year2.tsv	first_name, first_name	SQLITE	BUYER	FIRST_NAME	Direct Transformation, Direct Transformation
File, File	Contacts_year1.csv, Contacts_year2.tsv	last_name, last_name	SQLITE	BUYER	LAST_NAME	Direct Transformation, Direct Transformation
File, File	Contacts_year1.csv, Contacts_year2.tsv	email, email	SQLITE	BUYER	EMAIL	Direct Transformation, Direct Transformation
File, File	Contacts_year1.csv, Contacts_year2.tsv	car_make, car_make	SQLITE	BUYER	CAR_MAKE	Direct Transformation, Direct Transformation
File, File	Contacts_year1.csv, Contacts_year2.tsv	car_model, car_model	SQLITE	BUYER	CAR_MODEL	Direct Transformation, Direct Transformation
File, File	Contacts_year1.csv, Contacts_year2.tsv	car_color, car_color	SQLITE	BUYER	CAR_COLOR	Direct Transformation, Direct Transformation
File, File	Contacts_year1.csv, Contacts_year2.tsv	car_year, car_year	SQLITE	BUYER	CAR_YEAR	Direct Transformation, Direct Transformation
File, File	Contacts_year1.csv, Contacts_year2.tsv	price, price	SQLITE	BUYER	PRICE	Direct Transformation, Direct Transformation
File, File	Contacts_year1.csv, Contacts_year2.tsv	date_purchased, date_purchased	SQLITE	BUYER	DATE_PURCHASED	Direct transformation with format YYYY-MM-DD, Transform format to YYYY-MM-DD

115

The result of the list is the same, and you can hand these off to your developers to build into the first iteration of your ETL process flow.

Data Migration Process Flow Design

Everything related to your design is coming together. With the STTM, you now can code much of the ETL scripts, but you'll also want to space the development in a way that makes sense. For example, you can't start to load your data into the database if there's no table to receive it; that part would have to come first. Documenting the sequence of operations that you will perform is placed into the Data Migration Process Flow Design and serves as a great checklist to ensure the right parts are initiated when they need to be.

For our prototype, our Data Migration Process Flow is simple to graph and then describe (see Figure 6-5). For advanced migrations, it does require more thought, but the principles are the same.

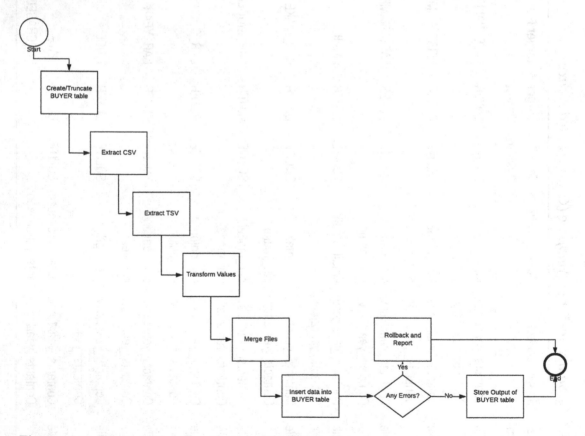

Figure 6-5. *Data Migration Process Flow Diagram*

In this list of steps, you'll see that we have thought about how we want our data to process between source and target; knowing what to add first; what to extraction, transformation, and loading; and then how to handle any exceptions. As with all our other documents, any last-minute additions or modifications can be appended to the model, directing our developers to make updates in their related code.

Development and Implementation

We now have a clear understanding of how our process flow will work, and, so far, we have not typed a single line of code. Finally, we've reached the point where our developers will take the technical contents of all the documents we've produced so far and will start writing the ETL scripts. Of course, work could have started after the STTM was complete, and any time-consuming transformations could have been researched in the earlier phases.

Note   In case you're curious, exactly how long from start to finish it takes to build this particular ETL script depends on several factors: the complexity of the transformations, the familiarity with the ETL tool and default scripting language, data accessibility, and any other number of variations we discussed in Chapter 5.

Assuming that the development team conducts daily stand-ups and peer reviews of code, let's assume that one sprint later (two weeks), they are ready to present you with a demonstration that will

1. Extract two files into PDI: the comma delimited and the tab delimited.

2. Transform the fields that require manipulation per the STTM.

3. Merge the resulting dataset.

4. Insert the final output into an SQLite solution.

Getting Ready

The script itself has already been written, so all you will need to do is test it. Even with that boost, you'll still have to perform some steps to get your system ready for testing:

- Clone the GitHub directory to your local computer.

- Download and install Pentaho Data Integration (PDI) Community Edition.

Clone the GitHub Directory

You'll need to have GitHub installed on your machine. See `https://gist.github.com/derhuerst/1b15ff4652a867391f03`[2] for instructions.

- The location you'll want to clone is at *https://github.com/Apress/building-a-data-integration-team.git*.

- The files you'll be using will be stored in the "chapter6" folder. Ensure that when you extract, you have three folders created: *input*, *output*, and *scripts*.

Download and Install PDI (Community Edition)

To accomplish this step, perform the following:

1. Go to the web site at *https://community.hitachivantara.com/s/article/data-integration-kettle*.

2. Read the section "How to get PDI up and running" based on your particular operating system (Linux, Windows, macOS).

3. Under Downloads, select the latest stable version.

4. Wait for the download to start.

5. Save the .zip file to a directory that you will remember. NOTE: The Pentaho download will leave a large footprint of 1 GB. Make sure your computer can support this file.

6. Once finished, unzip the package.

---

[2]"Installing Git on Linux, Mac OS X and Windows." 2019. *Gist*. `https://gist.github.com/derhuerst/1b15ff4652a867391f03`

7. In the new directory, under "data-integration," double-click the file spoon.sh (Linux), spoon.bat (Windows), or the "Data Integration" application icon (macOS). You should see the splash window open. Wait for the application to load.

Note   If the file does not run on Windows, ensure that you have Java JDK installed and added to your JAVA_HOME system variable. Go to *https://www. oracle.com/technetwork/java/javase/downloads/index.html* to download the latest version and confirm the JAVA_HOME environment variable is correctly set by clicking the Windows Start icon and searching for "Edit System Environment Variables."

---

8. Since this is your first time using the application, you will be presented with the Welcome window. Click File/New or (CTRL+N) to open a new transformation window (see Figure 6-6).

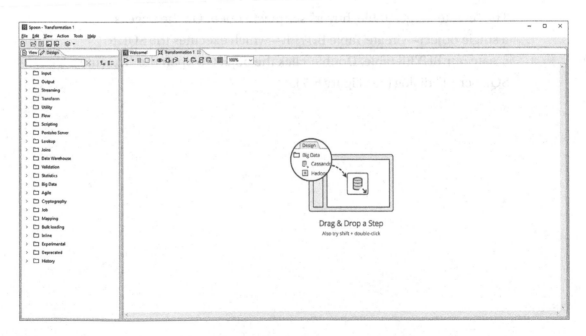

Figure 6-6. *A New PDI Transformation*

Note   We've chosen to use SQLite as our target database because it is a small, self-contained SQL Server engine that is open source and already operational with the PDI platform. It is different from most SQL databases in that SQLite does not have a separate server process and writes directly to ordinary disk files (*https://www.sqlite.org/about.html*)[3]. You won't have a client application to read the infomotors.db data, but you will have Pentaho scripts that will allow you to read the file, thereby serving the same purpose.

Opening the "create_target_table_buyer" Script

Although we won't be discussing how the downloaded scripts were developed, we can continue our walkthrough as if we were going to peer-review the code our developers created. For starters, while in PDI, click the File/Open menu (CTRL+O on Windows) and navigate to the chapter6\scripts directory that you cloned from GitHub. Double-click the file "create_target_table_buyer.ktr".

- The "create_target_table_buyer" script will open. On the page is a single object—Create Table BUYER—which executes the SQL to create our BUYER table. Double-click the object to open the "Execute SQL Script" dialog (see Figure 6-7).

---

[3]"About Sqlite." 2019. *Sqlite.org.* www.sqlite.org/about.html

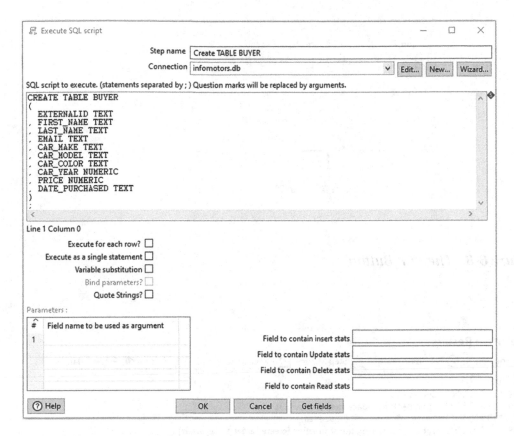

Figure 6-7. *The Execute SQL Script*

- In the "SQL script to execute" window (center of the screen), you'll see the CREATE TABLE STATEMENT that our developers added. Above that is a text box labeled "Connection." The value "infomotors. db" represents the connection to our SQLite target that we've built for our prototype. Click Edit if you want to see the details of the connection as well as the other out-of-the-box connectors that PDI provides. When you finish your review, click Cancel twice to return to the "Create target BUYER table" home page.

- At the top of the screen is a play button (see Figure 6-8). Click it to open the Run Options dialog box. Then click the Run button in that window to create the BUYER table (you can see the output results as shown in Figure 6-9).

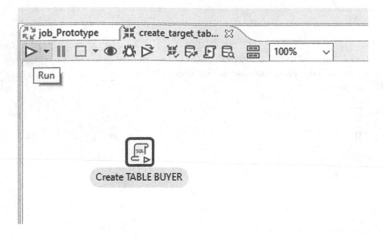

Figure 6-8. *The Run Button*

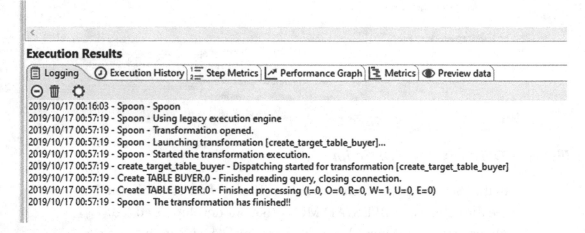

Figure 6-9. *Confirm That the Step Ran Successfully*

- Once completed, select File/Close from the menu (CTRL+W on
  Windows) to be returned to the main window.

Opening the "Prototype" Script

With the BUYER table created, we can now review the ETL script that does the bulk of
our work. To refresh our memories, here is the approach we took in our Data Migration
Process Flow:

1. Create/Truncate BUYER Table: Using the ETL tool, create the
   BUYER table if it does not already exist. If it does exist, then
   truncate all data to provide the next load.

2. Extract CSV: Using the ETL tool CSV connector, retrieve all comma-delimited data.

3. Extract TSV: Using the ETL tool text connector, retrieve all tab-delimited data.

4. Transform Values: Using the STTM as a reference, change the transformation values identified.

5. Merge Files: Combine the new (transformed) staging files into one file prepped for the target format.

6. Insert Data into BUYER Table: Using the ETL tool SQLite connector, insert all values into the BUYER table.

7. Decision: Were there any errors during load?

   a. If yes, then roll back the data and send a report.

   b. If no, then end the event.

We just covered part of Step 1 in the preceding text. Let's analyze another by opening the script *prototype.ktr*.

- As you did earlier with the *create_target_table_buyer* step, click the File/Open menu (CTRL+O on Windows) and navigate to the chapter6\scripts directory that you cloned from GitHub. Double-click the file "prototype.ktr." The script will open (see Figure 6-10).

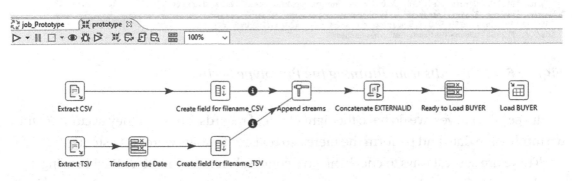

Figure 6-10. *The Prototype Script*

There's a lot more to deal with on this transformation than in the previous scenario, and we won't try to explain it in detail (if you do have the interest, there are several recommended books on Pentaho development, and Hitachi Vantara likewise has some excellent online help documents). If you follow the labels, it should look correct: we start by extracting our CSV and TSV files (Steps 2 and 3 from our Data Migration Process Flow), transform our TSV date field (Step 4), add a concatenated field that will serve as the EXTERNALID (also Step 4), append the finalized streams together (Step 5), and then load the data into the BUYER table (Step 6). If you want to explore what each of these functions does in your own Pentaho script, feel free to test it. Just make sure to click Cancel on each dialog box you open to avoid modifying any script components.

We're just about done, so all we need to do is test our script. But how can we do that? Earlier, we pressed the icon in the top-left corner (Run), so let's try executing again by clicking that same icon.

If you look at your Logging window (see Figure 6-11), you can see that we did indeed populate the BUYER table with 200 written records (W=200 means "write").

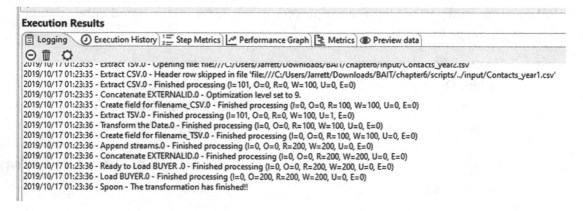

Figure 6-11. *Results from Running the Prototype Script*

It seems that, yes, we do have the right count of records, but were they accurate? Did we modify the date and perform the merge so that our formats were consistent?

There are several ways to check this. We could select from the BUYER table using another script (we do this in the next chapter), or we could right-click any of the steps on the prototype script and select "Preview" to see how the data reads at that particular point. Another way is by choosing the Preview Data tab, which is a few tabs to the right of the "Logging" option. Let's click that tab now (see Figure 6-12).

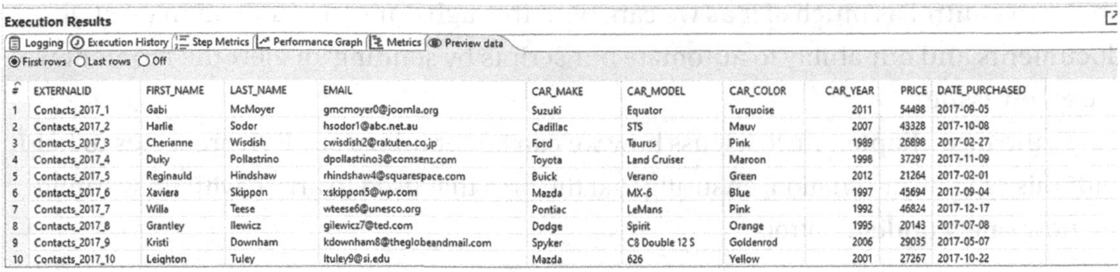

Execution Results

Logging | Execution History | Step Metrics | Performance Graph | Metrics | Preview data

First rows ○ Last rows ○ Off

#	EXTERNALID	FIRST_NAME	LAST_NAME	EMAIL	CAR_MAKE	CAR_MODEL	CAR_COLOR	CAR_YEAR	PRICE	DATE_PURCHASED
1	Contacts_2017_1	Gabi	McMoyer	gmcmoyer0@joomla.org	Suzuki	Equator	Turquoise	2011	54498	2017-09-05
2	Contacts_2017_2	Harlie	Sodor	hsodor1@abc.net.au	Cadillac	STS	Mauv	2007	43328	2017-10-08
3	Contacts_2017_3	Cherianne	Wisdish	cwisdish2@rakuten.co.jp	Ford	Taurus	Pink	1989	26898	2017-02-27
4	Contacts_2017_4	Duky	Pollastrino	dpollastrino3@comsenz.com	Toyota	Land Cruiser	Maroon	1998	37297	2017-11-09
5	Contacts_2017_5	Reginauld	Hindshaw	rhindshaw4@squarespace.com	Buick	Verano	Green	2012	21264	2017-02-01
6	Contacts_2017_6	Xaviera	Skippon	xskippon5@wp.com	Mazda	MX-6	Blue	1997	45694	2017-09-04
7	Contacts_2017_7	Willa	Teese	wteese6@unesco.org	Pontiac	LeMans	Pink	1992	46824	2017-12-17
8	Contacts_2017_8	Grantley	Ilewicz	gilewicz7@ted.com	Dodge	Spirit	Orange	1995	20143	2017-07-08
9	Contacts_2017_9	Kristi	Downham	kdownham8@theglobeandmail.com	Spyker	C8 Double 12 S	Goldenrod	2006	29035	2017-05-07
10	Contacts_2017_10	Leighton	Tuley	ltuley9@si.edu	Mazda	626	Yellow	2001	27267	2017-10-22

Figure 6-12. *The Preview Data Tab*

In this window, you can see all your records in one spreadsheet-like view. What we are seeing is the data just as it loaded into the BUYER table. If you scroll through the entire recordset, you'll notice that our EXTERNALID field follows the syntax we specified in our STTM, as does the DATE_PURCHASED format. It looks like the prototype was a success. Start handing out those Starbucks gift cards to your developers who worked hard to meet these requirements.

At this point, we've gone through a semi-implementation procedure. If this were an actual deliverable and not just a prototype, we would populate our Migration Results Report with the name of the object (BUYER), the date we ran our test, the total number of records executed, any errors we encountered, and other items suitable for iterative cleanup. Then it would be time for deployment to the next environment. Of course, let's not get ahead of ourselves.

Summary

If you've followed along, you'll see that our project passed all the tests. It seems like we are ready for Go-Live signoff. That's not surprising given that the scope of our migration was rather small. For much larger projects, however, monitoring all aspects of the ETL lifecycle can be more challenging, especially where testing and deployment are concerned. For example, at the last minute, database developers may make a change that impacts the integration teams' hardcoded scripts; or, even worse, code that worked fine with a testbed of data now throws strange errors when inserting into Production. Although we may not be able to predict these issues, we do have the ability to control as much of it as we can, both through our communication through documents and our ability to automate our scripts by sending an alert the moment we see a new issue.

In the next chapter, we'll discuss how we can better utilize our ETL processes to help with this type of automation, ensuring that the fires that used to arrive with no warning are now safely under control.

CHAPTER 7

Platform Automation

Software testers always go to heaven; they've already had their fair share of hell.

—Anonymous[1]

Introduction

I've repeated many times throughout this book how we often view data migration as a one-button operation—just select your source fields, push a button, and off you go, data migrated. By this point, I hope you realize that nothing is further from the truth. Data migration takes careful planning, days and perhaps weeks of research, and a wealth of collaboration via documentation, compromises, and meetings, all of which is the opposite of pushing a button.

After clarifying that, I'd now like to teach you how to design your integration systems so you can just push a button to run your complete integration from start to finish.

Yes, you read me right—one mouse click to test your jobs, retrieve your results, and deploy your system into different environments.

Don't get me wrong. All the steps I have described throughout this book are still valid. You will have to slog through the requirements, build your migration plans and STTM, and struggle to make your iterative ETL code work. But toward the end, when you finally have a working model, you can combine your scripts and establish a system that will run on demand or at a schedule you choose. In this chapter, we'll talk about the different types of environments in which you'll be working, preparing your scripts for automation, modifying your documents, demonstrating successes and errors, and the

---

[1] "Software Testing Quotes—Software Testing Fundamentals." 2019. *Software Testing Fundamentals.* http://softwaretestingfundamentals.com/software-testing-quotes/

127

steps for setting up a scheduled task. While not everything we discuss will be a one-click approach, we'll certainly get close enough to remove the mundane, time-consuming, and risky activities that accompany manual delivery.

If we're ready to go, let's start with a discussion on platform environments.

All About Environments

Why It Matters

When we have a deadline to meet and our project sponsor is asking us when we're going to have the iteration deployed, the last thing we're thinking about is something that's going to take *more time*. We want to get our code pushed into the Production server and move on to the next activity. We've tested as much as we can, reviewing the row counts and making sure the data looks fine, so let's move on. We reason it like this: If we find errors, it won't be the end of the world, and we can always patch post-deployment. Like the famous footwear commercial says, "Just do it."[2]

That sounds fine in principle and is usually the default tactic many professionals prefer when under the gun ("If I only had more time, I would do this the right way, but I don't, so I won't"). And this may even work. But with a process that depends on data accuracy, like integration, pushing bad code to production won't work for very long. This obstruction is due to a phenomenon called technical debt that I'll define as "the effort required to refactor/fix your code over time due to prioritizing speedy delivery over quality."[3] For example, you may have added hardcoded logic in a system because it passed your internal tests (let's use a pattern like "If the value equals 'IBM,' 'I.B.M,' or 'International Business Machines,' then convert to 'IBM Corp'"). Very pleased with yourself, you push your code from your local environment into Production and move on to the next task.

Several weeks later, you get an email from your target data owner that there's a new acronym, "I.B.M. Corporation," and it's creating confusion among the reporting systems. Okay, so you reopen your development code, make the hardcoded change, and push right back into Production. Took maybe 5 minutes, right?

---

[2] www.nike.com

[3] "What Is Technical Debt? Definition and Examples." 2019. *Productplan.com*. www.productplan.com/glossary/technical-debt/

Oh, but wait, it's really "IBM Corporation" with no periods between the I, B, and M. Dang, we should have caught that. Back to the Development system, adding this exception as well. Another 5 minutes, but not a big deal.

Until it is. Several weeks later, as all the additional exceptions start to roll in, the data owners admit that they are frustrated. You think and consider that maybe what you can build is a function that would pass parameters directly into a lookup table that would then provide the values for you with immediate results. Thus, instead of having to resubmit your entire codebase into Production every time your users report an error, they could simply add a physical exception record into a table (see Figure 7-1).

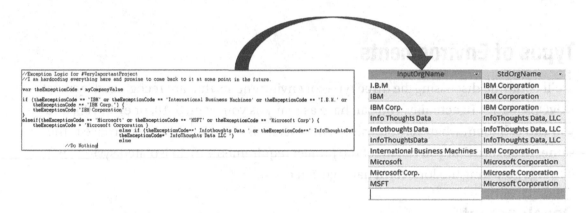

Figure 7-1. *Code Refactored to Lookup Table*

That's a good idea, right? Unfortunately, you've been using your laptop to develop some other functionality, and you're not sure if you still have the original code. If you're using Git or another version control system, you'll probably have to stash your existing code, roll back to your Production-deployed version, and then start refactoring each of your objects. It's progress, but do you honestly have time for that? Isn't there a better way to handle this?

You see where I'm going with this. What started as a quick workaround ended up costing you more time and effort (technical debt) in the long run. And despite your attempts to do the contrary, you now have a buggy piece of software you'll have to babysit alongside frustrated data owners.

Logically, we know that perfection is an illusion, and to be honest, you can never truly reduce technical debt (at least not permanently). But there are ways to manage it.[4] Our concern with technical debt is more for the repeatable process associated with nightly integrations rather than the one-time migration. One way to mitigate the pain associated with technical debt is by deploying your build strategically across the different environments using version control systems.

A few steps are involved in accelerating your nightly integration turnarounds. If you follow the techniques that I recommend throughout this chapter, the benefits you'll gain in productivity strongly outweigh the time it takes to do the environment planning and setup.

Types of Environments

We'll continue discussing the three types of environments that are recognized by most DevOps teams. In actuality, you can have as many as you want, 5, 10, or even 100, and you can call them whatever you want. It may seem like overkill, but the purpose is the same: to ensure that you can meet the project requirements in an isolated system, where, if things go wrong, no long-term damage can occur.

Development

Development (or "Dev") is the environment that's on your computer and where you initially update your code. It's where you download your prototype scripts and perform commits and may or may not exist on a remote server where your coworkers can produce separate versions of the data. This environment rapidly changes and, recalling children playing in a sandbox at recess, is sometimes referred to as a "sandbox."

The Development environment will allow the team to perform various experiments and should have connectivity with mock code or testing databases with non-production data. Any significant disruptions to the data that occur from testing are minimized, affecting only the users who are performing the intended operations.

---

[4]"There Are 3 Main Types of Technical Debt. Here's How to Manage Them." 2019. *Hackernoon. com*. https://hackernoon.com/there-are-3-main-types-of-technical-debt-heres-how-to-manage-them-4a3328a4c50c

Staging

The Staging environment is where most of our team reviews and Quality Assurance (QA) testing will happen, and we, therefore, want the staging environment to be as closely replicated to Production as possible, including the data housed in the source and target systems. For security or other technical reasons, you may not be allowed to store that type of snapshot information, but the closer you can get to a Production image, the more prepared you'll be for the actual Go-Live.

Configuring the Staging platform may seem like an arduous task, especially if there are a lot of hoops to jump through to request the various services you'll need as part of Production replication. But having this environment in a ready state means that you can test a faux system in isolation, knowing that any data issues you run into can be resolved through iteration and careful review rather than rapid-fire updates as might occur in Production.

You can build and test automation scripts here as well. This environment will allow you to work through multiple versions of your code, refining the loads to synchronize with the diagram you created for your Data Migration Process Flow. Most ETL tools support calling one task after another, and you can eventually align your workstream to run continuously in one step rather than manually executing one by one. While achieving this degree of automation is satisfying, I will admit that you can only get these results if the test data you are working within Staging is nearly the same as that in Production.

To replicate environments, some organizations I have worked with will take the existing Production environment and, following a deployment, will overwrite the Staging environment so that the latest and greatest version is available for use. By leveraging this, the Staging environment also becomes the platform by which you can accelerate your payback of technical debt; if we want to rewrite our code to reference a table instead of a script, we can work directly in the Staging platform to make a change. If using a version control system (VCS) such as Git, we can clone the master branch to be a new release. Either way, we will have the ability to pivot when we encounter bugs, deploy and test within a Production-like environment, and not miss a beat when we get that inevitable alert that something has failed.

Production

The Production environment represents the lifeblood of every creative endeavor that goes into a project from each code update to test result. It is where the distributed build lives and, for that reason, should only be touched when releasing a new version to users. Otherwise, customers will discover any issues that occur due to shoddy software design, and companies will lose both their money and their reputation if the problems are big enough.

Because of its openness to the public, deployment of buggy software should be kept under tight control, with the ability to release left only to a select few. Any planned deployments should be announced to parties well ahead of schedule (at least two weeks before) and include the time, date, and impact to simultaneously running processes. Release managers should also send emails the day of deployment to communicate when the rollout will begin and then, post-deployment, that it has finished.

Environments for One-Time Migration

Our ETL applications and corresponding scripts count as a build tool and should follow the same environmental structure as other software, that is, replicated each time for the Development, Staging, and Production platforms. However, one-time migration environments—applications and scripts that will only run once, migrating source data to target data for initialization—may only need to be created for a short time if teams allow it.

The typical ETL architecture contains a source, an ETL middleware, and a target. This architecture is illustrated in Figure 7-2.

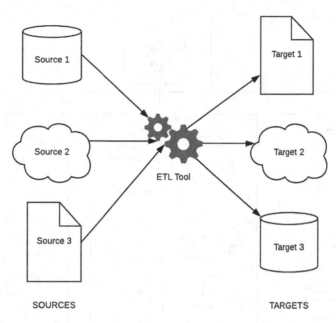

Figure 7-2. *A Typical ETL Architecture*

In the one-time migration architecture, rather than replicating the ETL tool across all platforms, we create only one instance, called the ETL Staging. The only requirement for operating this instance is that we update the connection endpoints to each of the individual environments during our deployments. By using this technique, the ETL Staging serves as a loosely coupled system with all the benefits you would expect from that design, such as improved testability, less maintenance of code, and increased scalability (see Figure 7-3).[5]

---

[5]"What Is Loose Coupling?—Dzone Integration." 2019. *Dzone.com.* https://dzone.com/articles/what-is-loose-coupling

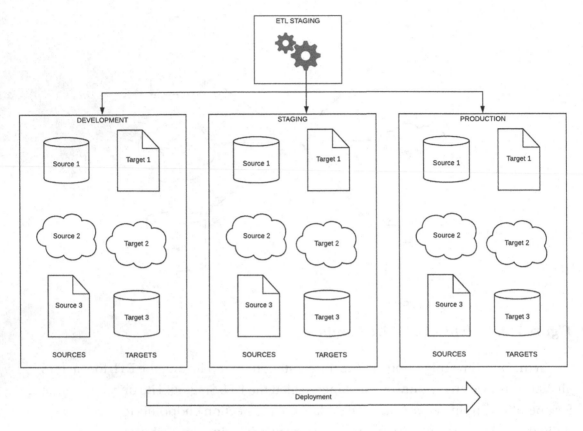

Figure 7-3. *One-Time Migration Model*

Again, this use of the one-time model rests upon the decisions of the organization and security teams. Often, the platform housing the ETL tool might be an internal Virtual Machine (VM). If you have not cleared those VMs to touch production data, then you would indeed have to replicate your application and corresponding scripts into a more secure environment, like that shown for repeatable integrations (see Figure 7-4).

Environments for Repeatable Integrations

The repeatable integration is a special kind of beast in that it both (a) points to a specific source and target endpoint and (b) is itself a script that requires different versions. If you recall, a repeatable integration is one that continuously updates data based on a web service trigger or scheduled time, such as once per evening, once per week, or once per month. These are less load intensive than one-time migration feeds and usually less complex in structure. Yet they also occur more frequently in organizations and require monitoring and operational support should any issues be detected.

Depending on their structure, the ETL tools associated with repeatable integrations will need to be installed on specialized VMs and released into their corresponding environments (Development, Staging, and Production) alongside any other software builds ready for deployment (see Figure 7-4).

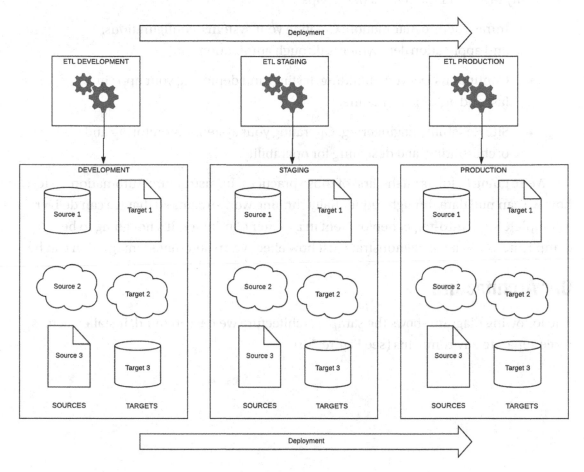

Figure 7-4. *Repeatable Integration Architecture*

DevOps Practices: A Sample Deployment

So far, we've focused on environments, architecture, and deployment. What, you may ask, does any of this have to do with platform automation (the title of this chapter)? Well, to start discussing automation, we're going to briefly touch upon DevOps, which has automation as one of its core goals.

According to Ernest Mueller, blogger for *The Agile Admin*, DevOps is defined as "the practice of operations and development engineers participating together in the entire service lifecycle, from design through the development process to production support."[6] He admits this is a rather broad definition and clarifies the following three practices that we usually discuss in the context of DevOps:

- Infrastructure Automation: Creating your systems, configurations, and application deployments through automation code

- Continuous Delivery: Building, testing, and deploying your apps in a fast and automated manner

- Site Reliability Engineering: Operating your systems, monitoring and orchestrating, and designing for operability

We're going to focus on the first of those practices, Infrastructure Automation, to test how we can pull data through sequentially running workstreams so that we can deliver a complete source-to-target deployment in a matter of minutes. It's not going to be complicated, and it will demonstrate just how effective an automated integration can be.

Our Architecture

The following diagram shows the sample architecture we have in mind, installed across three separate environments (see Figure 7-5).

---

[6]Mueller, Ernest. 2019. "What Is Devops?" *The Agile Admin*. https://theagileadmin.com/what-is-devops/

Orchestration Engine
or Scheduling Tool

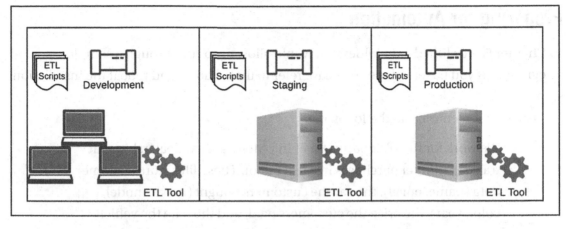

Figure 7-5. *ETL Design for Platform Automation*

What you see in Figure 7-5 is a sample design of how our ETL tool would operate across each of the different environments we've discussed. New to this diagram is the label for *Orchestration Engine/Scheduling Tool,* a software application that coordinates the sequencing of steps and activities according to a defined business process model.[7] An orchestration engine can be part of a software package or installed externally, as with Jenkins, an open source automation tool that continuously builds and tests software projects.[8] If a tool like Jenkins is not available, then we could substitute by using scheduling tools like Microsoft Task Scheduler, crontab for Mac, or cron for Linux.

Consider this architecture a logical representation, however. To simplify things, we're only going to install one instance of the ETL tool (the PDI from the previous chapter) on the local computer. Also, the three environments are different path names and not separate VMs. Regardless, this type of structure should be enough to simulate the kind of partitioning we're trying to achieve.

---

[7]"Orchestration Engine | Enterprise Architecture Glossary | Orbus Software." 2019. *Orbussoftware. com.* www.orbussoftware.com/resources/glossary/o/orchestration-engine/

[8]"What Is Jenkins? | Jenkins for Continuous Integration | Edureka." 2019. *Edureka.* www.edureka. co/blog/what-is-jenkins/

In our demonstration, I'm using Windows and will forgo installing Jenkins instead of utilizing the built-in Task Scheduler. macOS and Linux users can follow along at their own pace or, if you're familiar with Jenkins, you can set up an experimental testbed.

Preparing for Automation

In Chapter 6, we cloned a Git folder that would allow us to run through a sample integration. If you haven't done so, please refer to that chapter and repeat the installation steps.

The initial scenario was the following:

- We work for the IT department of InfoMotors, a car dealership that tracks customer purchases in a text editor. These files store customer data (name, email), the car the customers bought (make, model, color, year), the price the customers paid, and the date the vehicle was purchased. Because InfoMotors is a new dealer, they do all their bookkeeping and reporting in Excel.

- But things are changing, and in order to improve their efficiency and minimize data issues, management would like to migrate their text files into a new on-premise database.

After sizing up the requirements and building out our Source-to-Target Mapping, we architected our Data Migration Process Flow Diagram and wrote our summary (see Figure 7-6):

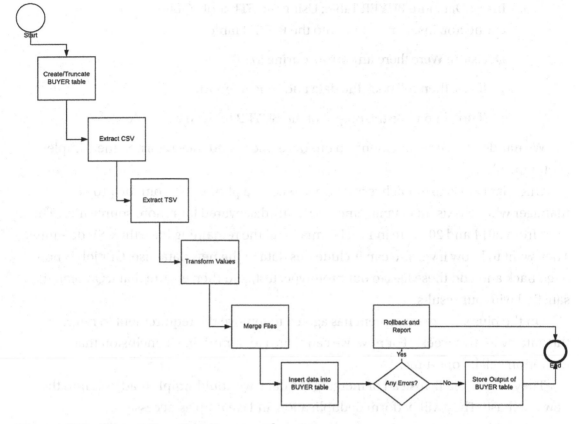

Figure 7-6. *Data Migration Process Flow Diagram*

1. Create/Truncate BUYER Table: Using the ETL tool, create the
    BUYER table if it does not already exist. If it does exist, then
    truncate all data to provide the next load.

2. Extract CSV: Using the ETL tool CSV connector, retrieve all
    comma-delimited data.

3. Extract TSV: Using the ETL tool text connector, retrieve all tab-
    delimited data.

4. Transform Values: Using the STTM as a reference, change the
    transformation values identified.

5. Merge Files: Combine the new (transformed) staging files into one
    file prepped for the target format.

139

6. Insert Data into BUYER Table: Using the ETL tool SQLite connector, insert all values into the BUYER table.

7. Decision: Were there any errors during load?

    a. If yes, then roll back the data and send a report.

    b. If no, then write the output of the BUYER table to a .csv file.

We handed these requirements to our developers, and they returned the completed prototype files.

One night close to our delivery date, we receive a phone call from the project manager who tells us that management recently discovered four more source files. The ones from 2014 and 2015 are in Excel format, and the remaining have the CSV delimiter. They want to know if we also can include this data in the new database. Our job is now to go back and add these files to our prototype, test, and then ensure that a QA team is satisfied with our results.

On the plus side, management has agreed to remove the requirement to migrate the data every two weeks. For now, we can return to our original conclusion that the migration will be one-time.

They also asked if, instead of merging the data, we could simply load as is into the new database. They will perform deduplication and cleanup as necessary.

Given this new information, we reiterate our process and reconvene the initiation phase. Taking each part at a time, you approach your integration team with the new requirements. "Can this be done?" you ask. "And how long will it take?"

The lead developer says, "It'll be hard work. But we'll do our best to have it done by the end of next sprint."

Note   I would suspect it's probably going to take less time than two sprints, but your lead developer won't tell you that as he wants to demonstrate the team's heroics by underpromising and overdelivering. Integration teams rock.

You have prepared your next steps. You go back and reopen the documents that had previously received approval, marking down the new requirements. For example, you change your earlier approach in the Data Migration Plan to resemble the following.

Proposed Migration and Integration Approach

Using an ETL tool, we will be extracting data from six files (three comma-delimited, one tab-delimited, and two Excel), performing transformations on the internal data to fit the target structure, and extracting to the target database. All data entry going forward will be delivered on the target system.

You can modify the future state diagram as well to represent the multiple CSV and XLS files rather than just the CSV and TSV from our first iteration (see Figure 7-7).

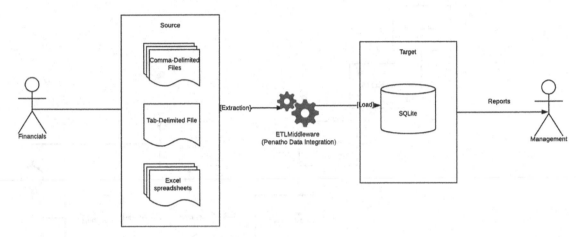

Figure 7-7. *Modified Future State*

All this is designed to communicate the strategy to the broader audience as well as confirm with anyone reviewing the documents that the assumptions are correct.

You'll reenter your discovery, design, and build phases in much the same manner. You'll redo profiling on the new datasets, you'll modify your STTM with the updated source-to-target fields and transformation rules, and you'll plug the latest steps into your Data Migration Plan. These activities are as simple as adding and removing the appropriate boxes to your flowchart and then adjusting your summary to match it (see Figure 7-8).

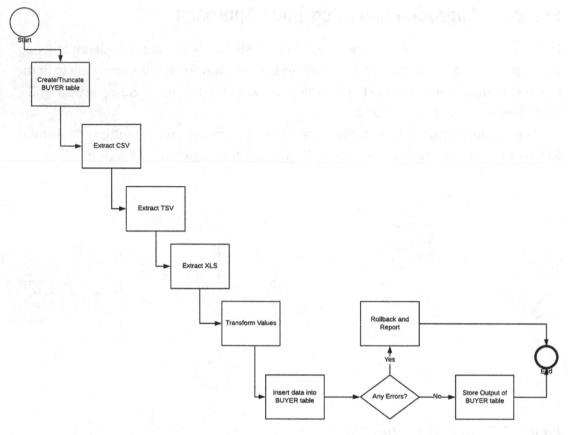

Figure 7-8. *Data Migration Process Flow Diagram (Updated)*

1. Create/Truncate BUYER Table: Using the ETL tool, create the BUYER table if it does not already exist. If it does exist, then truncate all data to provide the next load.

2. Extract CSV: Using the ETL tool CSV connector, retrieve all comma-delimited data.

3. Extract TSV: Using the ETL tool text connector, retrieve all tab-delimited data.

4. Extract Excel: Using the ETL tool text connector, retrieve all Excel spreadsheet data.

5. Transform Values: Using the STTM as a reference, change the transformation values identified.

6. Insert Data into BUYER Table: Using the ETL tool SQLite connector, insert all records into the BUYER table.

7. Decision: Were there any errors during load?

   a. If yes, then roll back the data and send a report.

   b. If no, then end the event.

You hand these modified documents to your development team and ask them to build you the latest and greatest version of the ETL. Just for kicks, and to keep with the theme of this chapter, you'll want them to automate the process so the data can extraction, transformation, and loading with a single mouse click.

Demonstration

The chapter7 folder contains the latest version of your data system, replicated in folders designed to be the development, staging, and production environments. After cloning the GitHub directory and installing Pentaho as written in Chapter 6, do the following:

- Depending on your OS, open the spoon.bat file (Windows), spoon.sh file (Linux), or Data Integration app shortcut (macOS).

- Click the File/Open menu (CTRL+O on Windows) and navigate to the chapter7\development\scripts directory that you downloaded from GitHub. Double-click the file "job_infomotors2.kjb". The script will open (see Figure 7-9).

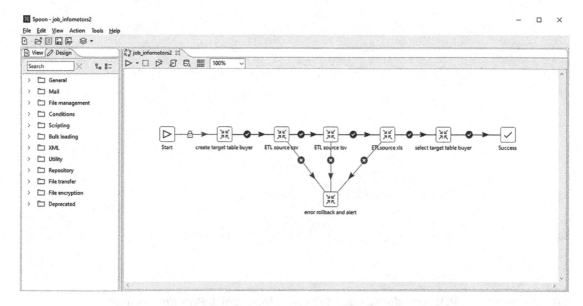

Figure 7-9. *The job_infomotors2.kjb Script*

What you are seeing is, in Pentaho parlance, known as a "job." It is like an orchestration engine in that it coordinates the execution and dependencies of your ETL tasks and activities.[9]

This job is the automation script we've been talking about and contains calls to the other ETL functions we identified in our Data Migration Process Flow. The window shows these tasks lined up by sequence:

- create target table buyer

- ETL source csv

- ETL source tsv

- ETL source xls

- select target table buyer

You'll notice there's also a task at the bottom of the page connected via the ETL tasks. This step is the failure "hop" that will trigger if any of the ETL processes fail, performing a rollback and alert on the type and nature of the error.

- If you right-click any of these steps and click "Open Referenced Object ➤ Transformation," you'll open the embedded script associated with that step. As we did in Chapter 6, let's do that with "create target table buyer" (see Figure 7-10).

[9]"Basic Concepts of PDI: Transformations, Jobs and Hops." 2019. *Pentaho Documentation.* https://help.pentaho.com/Documentation/7.0/0L0/0Y0/030/010

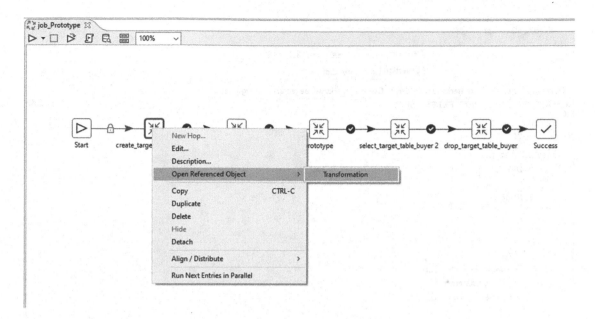

Figure 7-10. *Right-Click create target table buyer*

Note   As we discussed during our earlier demonstration, you can also open the scripts by clicking File/Open and selecting the appropriate name from the chapter6/scripts directory. The way I have designated by right-clicking takes fewer steps, but you can choose your specific preference.

You will see that this step is written similarly to the earlier iteration we worked with, except we've modified the SQL so that the table instantiates if it does not already exist. In other words, the first time you run this application, the development database schema (infomotors_dev.db) is created along with the BUYER table (see Figure 7-11).

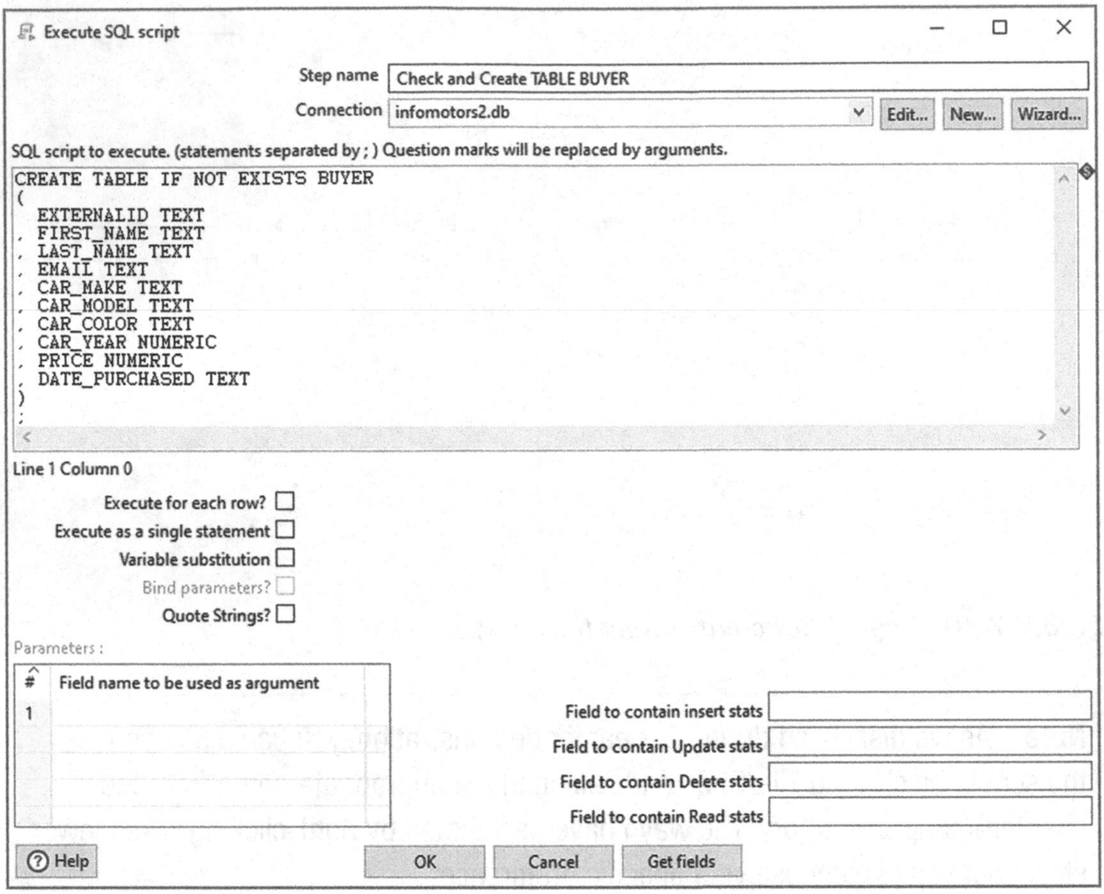

Figure 7-11. *Updated Version of CREATE TABLE BUYER*

- Because this script will run when we execute the job, you don't need to do anything. Click Cancel in this window and the job_infomotors tab at the top left of the window.

- Now, right-click the "ETL source csv" step, and select "Open Referenced Object" ➤ "Transformation." What you see is the model that extracts the (multiple) CSV files, transforms the data, and then loads into the BUYER table.

You will note that this file is different from the "prototype" script in that we've separated the tab-delimited step along with the new Excel step and put them into their separate processes. We could have incorporated them into one file, but it made sense from an architecting standpoint to separate them by keeping the functions modular and devoted to one specific duty.

- There are a few other patterns in the connector that we should review.

- To start, double-click the "Extract Multiple CSVs" to open it (see Figure 7-12).

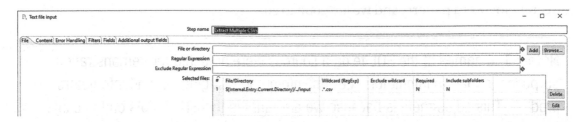

Figure 7-12. *Extract Multiple CSVs*

You will notice that where it says Selected Files, we have a directory path marked like this:

```
${Internal.Entry.Current.Directory}/../input
```

The value in between the *${...}* is a PDI internal variable. It tells us that the variable under scrutiny is the one where we have saved the script. On my machine, we have saved our job to directory *C:\Users\<<insert your username here>>\Documents\BAIT\chapter7\ development\scripts*. Yours should be similar. The /../ after the variable represents one level up, and the file input is the last directory value. Thus, I am performing a lookup against path *C:\Users\Jarrett\Documents\BAIT\chapter7\development\input,* which contains InfoMotors' sample records.

The next column is the Wildcard (RegEx), which indicates the filter of files to lookup, which, for this task, is .*.csv. That is, any file marked with suffix .csv and stored in the development\input directory will be read into the system.

What makes this structure particularly useful is that ANY file with a .csv prefix that we store in the \input directory will be read and automatically appended. Of course, the formats will need to match the input we're expecting to use (id, first_name, last_name, and so on), and some quick data profiling will help us determine if this is indeed the case.

Because we're using a variable for our input path rather than hardcoding it, we no longer have to know *where* we're storing our script. We just have to ensure that we have a one level up (/../) and an additional input path. This syntax is why we can quickly put this same script in a completely separate environment, and it will work as is, blind to the fact that its directory structure is different. For example, if you open the same "ETL source csv" file in our staging directory, you'll see we have the same file in use, except this time, our staging script is reading from the *staging* folder rather than from the *development* folder. This generic code is, to me, the secret sauce of deployment. No matter where we store this script, all we have to do is ensure the latter half of the directory follows a pattern, and we are good to go.

Note   The names of the SQLite data sources were adjusted for demonstration purposes to map to infomotors_dev.db, infomotors_staging.db, and infomotors_prod.db. This adjustment is because we are running the ETL scripts on the same machine and do not want to overwrite data that should be segregated. In a typical infrastructure, you would most likely be using the same database schema, tables, and fields, and this connector could remain hardcoded or, if you prefer, also as a variable.

I'll leave it to you to review the ETL source .tsv and the ETL source .xls scripts located on the job_infomotors job. You'll see they follow the same format, but with the Wildcard values adjusted to match their filters of .*.tsv and .*.xls. As with the CSV files, we can add any number of suffixed files to the */input* folder of that environment, and each one will be included in our job run.

The Output Step

We have two more steps to examine before we test the complete automation.

- In the job_infomotors page, right-click the "select target table buyer" step and select "Open Referenced Object ➤ Transformation." The process will open.

The purpose of this step is to meet the requirements specified in our Data Migration Process Flow which will serve as a sanity check when we test our job execution. Two activities are accomplished (see Figure 7-13).

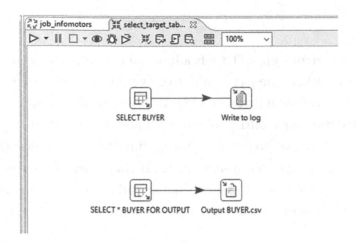

Figure 7-13. *The "select target table buyer" Process*

The first activity executes a "SELECT COUNT" on the InfoMotors BUYERS table. The PDI log displays this count for your review. The second SELECT retrieves all the fields of the BUYER dataset and delivers the results to a CSV file called "BUYER.csv." Similar to the inputs in our extraction steps, the output is pointing to your relative environment's / *output* directory (see Figure 7-14).

Step name	Output BUYER.csv
Filename	${Internal.Entry.Current.Directory}/../output/BUYER.csv
Pass output to servlet	☐
Create Parent folder	☑
Do not create file at start	☐
Accept file name from field?	☐
File name field	
Extension	
Include stepnr in filename?	☐
Include partition nr in filename?	☐
Include date in filename?	☐
Include time in filename?	☐
Specify Date time format	☐
Date time format	Specify Date time format
	Show filename(s)...
Add filenames to result	☑

Figure 7-14. *The BUYER.csv Output Directory*

Rollback

Our final step is the error step. ETL tools allow you to control how you want your exception logic to work. In the ETL world, two overall categories of errors can occur. The first is a Technical Error, and you will see this due to an issue on the network, infrastructure, or security side of the house. For example, a Technical Error is caught when you try to retrieve information from a database that is offline or when attempting to log into a system using an old password. In these situations, your ETL would be programmed to alert the network, infrastructure, or database administrators on the error cause, time, date, and any other information that would be helpful.

The second category is called a Business Error. This error happens if a workflow rule or requirement that was expected to occur does not. For example, if a field contains letters when it should provide only digits, a Business Error will be triggered. The IBM naming standard and workaround we discussed earlier in this book is another example of a Business Error, albeit one that would not set off alarms. Given the subjective extent to which data can be "wrong," Business Errors are often harder to resolve than technical glitches, and your team will spend a considerable amount of time trying to find new ways to eliminate data issues. Fortunately, your strategy of continuously improving your ETL logic, improving your deployments, and monitoring changes (see Chapter 8) will fall into place, and your team eventually will become crack sharpshooters in the area of data remediation.

For now, we'll keep the rollback strategy simple. Any error, be it Technical or Business, will cause our script to fire. Open the "error rollback and alert" step in the usual way, and you'll see that there are only two tasks: deleting all records from the BUYER table and sending a log alert to PDI with the message: `"An error occurred with the integration. Rolling back"` (see Figure 7-15).

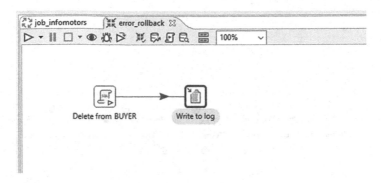

Figure 7-15. *The error rollback and alert Step*

Testing the Automation

With an understanding of the steps, it's now time to run our job from start to finish. Remember when I promised you the one-button click?

- On the job_infomotors main page, click the Run button. A "Run Options" page will open.

- Click Run on the "Run Options" page.

(Okay, you're probably saying that this was TWO button clicks. We're not quite finished in this chapter, so be patient.)

If all works as expected, your job flow should run through the entire process, start to finish. That is, we met the requirements stated in our Data Migration Process Flow and Source-to-Target Mapping and aligned with the purpose and future state of our Data Migration Plan. That is a lot to accomplish in just TWO button pushes.

If you review the Execution Results Logging pane, you'll see the different workstreams that fired along with the read and write counts, alerts, and duration. This log pane is a feature you'll use in PDI often, but any ETL system worth its cost will offer similar reporting standards (see Figure 7-16).

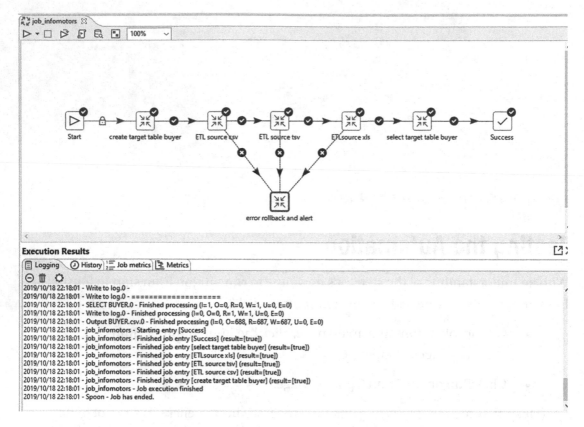

Figure 7-16. *Execution Results Logging Panel*

According to my log, we loaded 687 records just shy of 2 seconds. Not bad timing, despite that we are still one click too many.

If you want to view the records that we loaded and subsequently pulled from our database table, navigate over to "chapter7/development/output" and open the BUYER. csv file.

Testing

Before setting up our scheduled ETL, we have one last topic to discuss: testing. In the DevOps world, we should automate testing, and, to be truthful, it can involve some heavy-duty operations. Development and test automation engineers need to work together to develop test scripts, maximize test coverage of the coded scripts, and, by using a variety of CI/CD tools, generate test scripts, deploy them, and run them in a continuous cycle.[10]

Going headlong into automated testing is outside the scope of this book. Suffice to say, what we want to do is find a way to run our tests quickly and to ensure that we recover from them gracefully. To do that, we would want to extract data that causes Technical and Business Errors, and we could then observe how our system reacts to the issue. Ideally, this would all be done behind the scenes, using a Test environment, scripts, and data built for this purpose.

Instead of going through those motions, we're going to do our testing old school style by opening a CSV file in our input directory, changing one value in our data script to make it invalid, and rerunning our job. That's it. So if you're ready, do the following steps:

1. In your chapter7\development\input directory, open the file "Contacts_2016.csv" using Notepad or through a favorite word processor such as Sublime, Notepad++, Vim, or TextPad. I would avoid using Word, WordPad, or Excel since the change we want to make is minor, and these applications can add characters and strip off values when saving CSV files.

2. Change the last value on the second row to "ABCDE" (see Figure 7-17)

```
id,first_name,last_name,email,car_make,car_model,car_color,car_year,price,date_purchased
1,Naoma,Duckfield,nduckfield0@youtu.be,Merkur,XR4Ti,Purple,1985,93961,ABCDE
2,Casandra,Wallington,cwallington1@google.it,Isuzu,Space,Aquamarine,1994,88001,2016-10-24
3,Hedvige,Melpuss,hmelpuss2@usgs.gov,Chevrolet,Express 1500,Red,2009,67984,2016-06-05
4,Juana,Valentine,jvalentine3@cnet.com,Chevrolet,G-Series 2500,Turquoise,1998,94466,2016-07-05
5,Barth,Kraut,bkraut4@uol.com.br,BMW,M6,Red,2006,58063,2016-03-21
6,Crissy,Faithfull,cfaithfull5@dell.com,Buick,Riviera,Purple,1990,12474,2016-04-05
7,Juanita,Volant,jvolant6@washington.edu,Honda,Accord,Yellow,1997,79062,2016-11-30
8,Read,Brimm,rbrimm7@google.pl,Chevrolet,Express 1500,Pink,2012,59722,2016-05-05
9,Darby,Elsegood,delsegood8@ucoz.com,Oldsmobile,Cutlass Supreme,Turquoise,1995,60857,2016-06-22
```

Figure 7-17. Changing the CSV

3. In PDI, rerun the job_infomotors by clicking the Run button.

---

[10]"Test Automation: The Secret to Devops Success—Work Life by Atlassian." 2019. *Work Life by Atlassian*. www.atlassian.com/blog/devops/test-automation-secret-devops-success

If all works as expected, the process flow will start, but you will trigger an error on the "ETL source csv" step. The path shown on the screen will be directed toward the "error rollback and alert" step (see Figure 7-18).

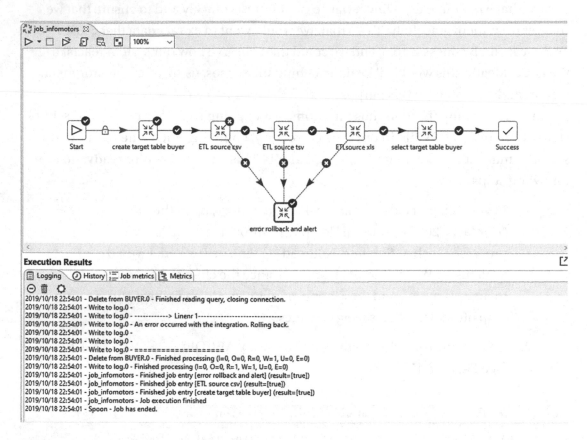

Figure 7-18. *ETL source csv Error*

The Execution Results Logging pane will show the output from your job. You should see the alert message we programmed ("An error occurred with the integration. Rolling back") as well as the steps that delete from the BUYER table.

If, at this point, you were to open the "select target table buyer" step and run this process manually, you would see from the log that the count of the table was zero, thereby confirming that the table is empty (see Figure 7-19).

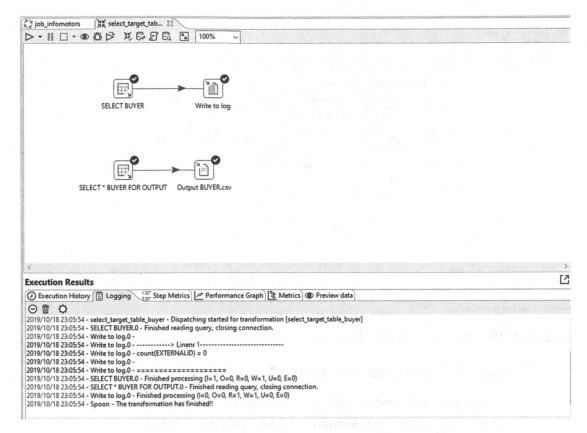

Figure 7-19. *Results from the Select Buyer Table Post-error. Notice the Count Equals 0*

Job Scheduling

As a final step, we're going to set this job to run on demand and on schedule. Earlier, I wrote about using orchestration engines like Jenkins or scheduling tools like Microsoft Task Scheduler for automating our scripts. In this step, we'll configure Task Scheduler to get our PDI job to execute every 5 minutes. As mentioned, feel free to explore testing the job executions using your preferred orchestration engine or scheduling tool.

1. Click the Windows Start icon and type the words "task scheduler." Press Enter.

    Task Scheduler will start (see Figure 7-20).

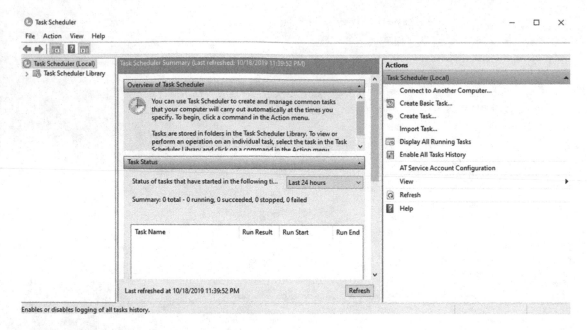

Figure 7-20. *Windows Task Scheduler*

2.   Select the action labeled "Create Task."

3.   The Create Task window will open (see Figure 7-21). On the General tab, enter the information in the fields provided:

- Name: Run Infomotors_ETL.

- Description: Whatever you prefer, but for knowledge transfer purposes, I will usually be clear and not leave this field empty.

- Check "Run with highest privileges."

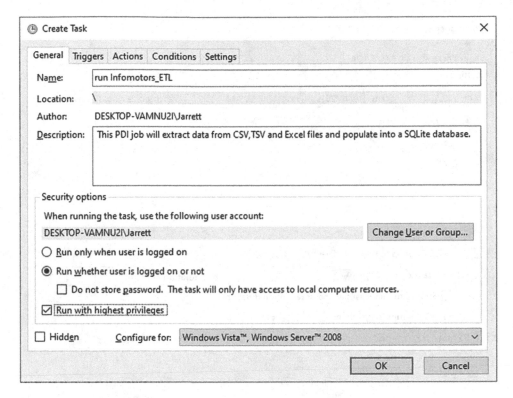

Figure 7-21. *The General Tab*

4. Under Triggers, click the New button. The New Trigger window
    will open (see Figure 7-22). Enter your details here. For example, I
    chose to repeat my task every 5 minutes, starting at midnight. You
    can choose whatever you like, of course, but preferably something
    that won't be more than an hour from the time you begin.

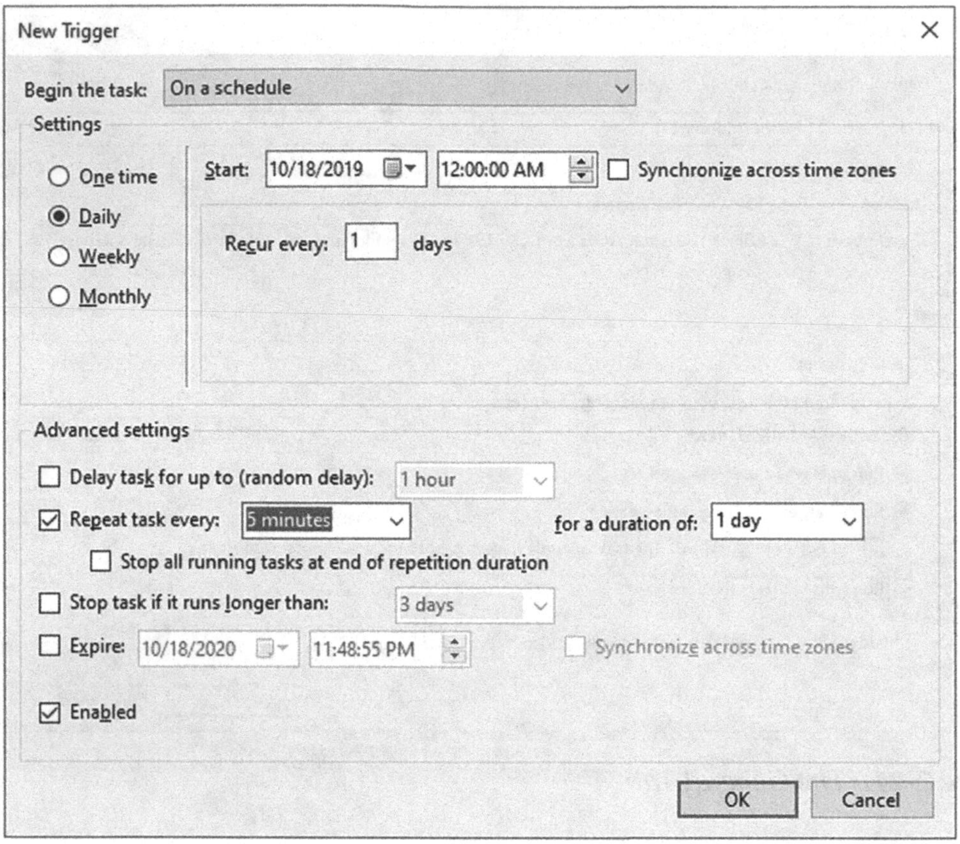

Figure 7-22. *New Trigger*

5. Under Actions, click the New button. The New Action window will open (see Figure 7-23). Enter your details exactly as you see here:

- Action: Start a program

- Program/script: <Path where you extracted Pentaho>\data integration\kitchen.bat

- Add arguments: /file:<Path where your script file is installed>\ job_infomotors.kjb

Most ETL tools include a command-line executable that will allow you to run your process through a single command. *Kitchen* is the PDI command-line tool for executing jobs. In the Add arguments field, you are selecting your job for execution (see Figure 7-23). Use whichever environment you want.

For more details on other parameters and command-line tools you can use with PDI, please reference *https://help.pentaho. com/Documentation/7.0/0L0/0Y0/070.*[11]

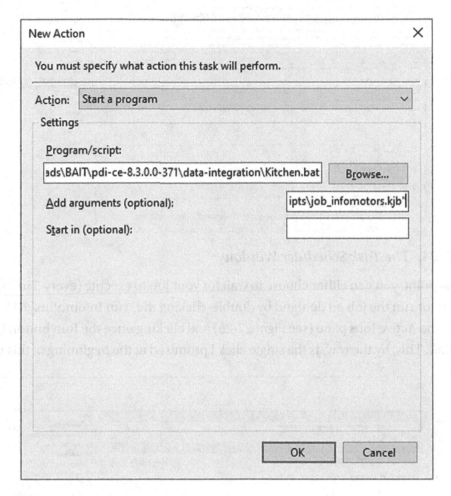

Figure 7-23. *New Action*

6. Click OK and OK again.

7. You may receive a request to authenticate your username and password credentials. Please do so at this time.

8. You will return to the Task Scheduler window (see Figure 7-24).

---

[11]"Use the Pan and Kitchen Command Line Tools to Work with Transformations and Jobs." 2019. *Pentaho Documentation.* https://help.pentaho.com/Documentation/7.0/0L0/0Y0/070

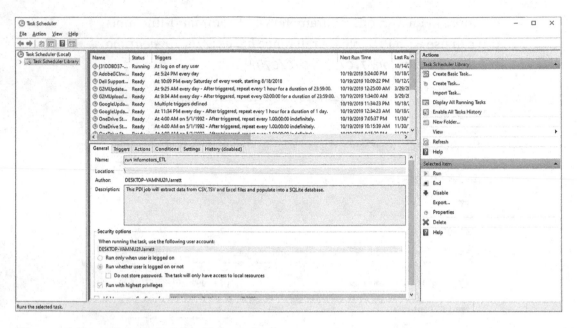

Figure 7-24. *The Task Scheduler Window*

At this point, you can either choose to wait for your job to execute (every 5 minutes in my case) or run the job on demand by double-clicking the "run Infomotors_ETL job" located in the Active Jobs pane (see Figure 7-25) and clicking once the Run button (see Figure 7-26). This, by the way, is the single click I promised at the beginning of this chapter.

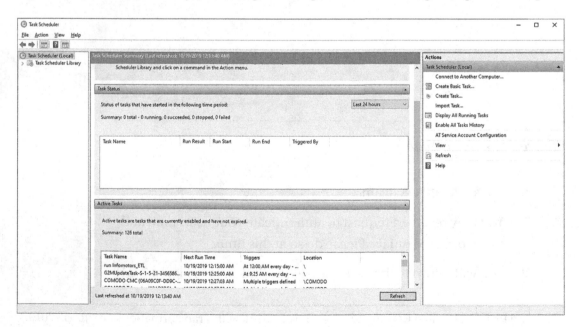

Figure 7-25. *Double-Click Active Tasks*

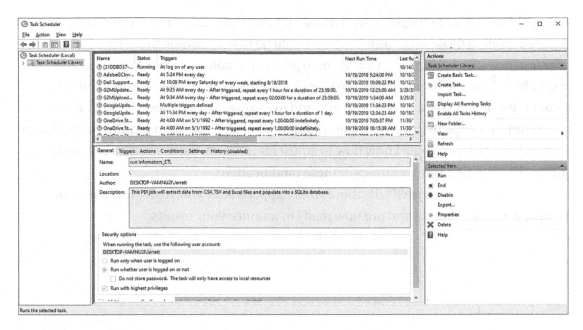

Figure 7-26. *Select the Run Button*

You can confirm the job has executed successfully by examining the upper pane of the Task Scheduler, searching for your activity, and scrolling to the Last Run Result.

This final confirmation may not be enough for you, and you may be wondering what else there is. There's a lot you can do, most of it based on the customer requests for success and error handling. For example, with many of the integrations we deliver, we configure emails to be distributed on both successful completion and failure. Furthermore, instead of entering the ETL command-line interface (CLI) tool in the New Action window as we did in our example, our teams often prefer to call a wrapper script that triggers the ETL CLI activity, thereby keeping the code easier to modify should we change tools or processes. These are just a few of the things you can do with your scheduled jobs, and your ETL tools should have the ability to support much more.

Summary

This chapter has introduced you into the world of deployment, automation, and scheduling. After learning some of the distinctions among Development, Staging, and Test platforms, we demonstrated how we could configure our prototype to be flexible to work in any environment, adaptable to include as many file types as needed, and repeatable to be set to trigger every 5 minutes. Most of the ETL products on the market today, as well as those built from scripts, should be able to handle these types of contingencies, so I encourage your team to go out and continue the research of what works best. The gold is not in the tool itself but in the ability of the chosen application to handle whatever data is thrown at you and to resolve those issues with increased acceleration. I hope that you now feel confident enough that, when requirements change in the eleventh hour, you'll know how to adjust rapidly and, more importantly, look forward to the speed and accuracy of these modifications.

In the next chapter, we'll talk about what happens after you've deployed to your Production environment and are now ready to monitor your results.

CHAPTER 8

Monitoring Results

We're rapidly entering a world where everything can be monitored and measured. But the big problem is going to be the ability of humans to use, analyze, and make sense of the data.

—Erik Brynjolfsson[1]

Introduction

At last, we've gotten through the ordeal of discovery, designing, testing, and deployment. We know our data inside and out, we've alerted teams to discrepancies, and we've managed to automate (as much as we can) the one-time migration and repeatable integrations. We've even set up an alerting system when we run into Business Rules and Technical Errors. What's left?

Fortunately (or unfortunately, depending on your perspective), the work of an integration team is never done. Post-deployment, we now enter the crucial phase of monitoring in which we work with the target data team to resolve their data issues, ensure that we've refactored unique errors still encountered by the ETL process, and review the daily and weekly logs for statistics that will allow the enterprise to improve their data goals. These activities are an incremental process, and the clock starts to tick the day after deployment. Let's begin from that first day, noting the milestones and issues that are liable to crop up.

---

[1]"Erik Brynjolfsson Quotes—Brainyquote." 2019. *Brainyquote.* www.brainyquote.com/authors/erik-brynjolfsson-quotes

Day One: Post-deployment

That first day after the migration is liable to be a busy one. On the one hand, you eagerly want to share in the celebrations, but on the other hand, there's a new application chock full of data, and users are ready to access. If you're on the front lines of help desk support, you'll be getting one call after another from users wondering if this record was sent or that value was brought over because it no longer exists or it exists but in a different format or it never existed and now it has miraculously appeared. With all the potential for a disruptive day, how will your team handle this surge?

Well, the good news is they may not have to. At least, not initially. The integration team is on the hook for handling data issues related to the migration process, but there are a few checkpoints that these requests will have to get through first. You'll need to establish your level of support within your organization, the topic we'll cover next.

Level of Support

Unless you work for a smaller company with scarce resources, the integration team is not typically on the front end of the help desk support. For midsize to large organizations, there will usually be a stratification of the roles used to handle bugs and similar complaints, and the integration team will be shielded from the majority of them (see Figure 8-1). Blogger Joe Hertvik has written a primer on the different levels of support:[2]

| Level 0: Automated Support | Level 1: Basic Support and Troublehsooting | Level 2: User device support | Level 3: Infrastructure support | Level 4: Vendor support |

Figure 8-1. *Levels of Help Desk Support*

---

[2]Hertvik, Joe. 2019. "Help Desk Management: What Is Level 1, Level 2, and Level 3 Help Desk Support?" *Joe Hertvik: Tech Machinist.* https://joehertvik.com/help-desk-definitions-level-1-level-2-level-3-support/

- Level 0 Support: Online, telephone, or similar self-service solutions that users can access themselves without the aid of additional support. For your integration, the types of calls you would expect at this level are those users who need to reset their password or who want access to a knowledge base to clarify how the new rollout affects their old data.

- Level 1 Support: This level filters the inbound help desk calls and provides essential support and troubleshooting. The Level 1 technician will gather and analyze user issues and determine the next steps, such as determining if this is a duplicate issue with a previous fix, ticket routing, and escalation to Level 2 or Level 3 support. Level 1 support will often be the front line for any of the complaints coming in about the integration product and process and should be given a list of instructions for common questions that have immediate responses, such as explaining a new Search-By-Name feature that has replaced a Search-By-Id feature. Level 1 support also should know about your Production downtimes (see Production issues) and have the detailed information at hand if callers are having network-related issues.

- Level 2 Support: In some organizations, Level 2 support is reserved for user device support such as laptops, desktops, and tablets, but may also share work with Level 3. Level 2 handles any complaints that are device related such as configuration issues, troubleshooting, software installations, and hardware repair. They receive the frontline requests from Level 1 support and, depending on how the help desk operates its own skillset or abilities, may need to escalate further onto Level 3. Some examples of how the integration project would affect Level 2 support would be if users required a specific product installed to access the reporting warehouse or wanted to request additional drive space to increase the amount of exported data.

- Level 3 Support: Level 3 is the support team responsible for configuring and fixing the server, network, file shares, and infrastructure issues. Level 3 tickets are most likely the ones your team will face as any integration and data movement questions fall into the realm of infrastructure. As these calls come in (usually through Level 1 or Level 2 escalation), you'll need to know important information for troubleshooting such as the records involved, which system or project was the user was logged into when the error happened, the error messages received (if any), and what results were expected. Because the team will want to prioritize issues that have the most significant impact, assessing the level of seriousness (Small, Medium, Large, Showstopper) will also be useful. Keep in mind that urgency from your user means that many of the issues you encounter will be designated as a Showstopper, even if reality claims otherwise.

- Level 4 Support: Although not commonly used as an internal help desk tier, Level 4 does have its place in the data integration world. Level 4 refers to your hardware and software vendors that have worked directly with your team or have a contract for a specific service. If the service ticket received by the Level 3 team is due to internal errors with the ETL software or other components outside your control, you may have to reach out to your vendor (Level 4) and work through the issue through their service desk. Issue resolution times should be set within the contract's Service-Level Agreement (SLA), and it's essential to keep your account representative's contact information available in case you're not getting the timely response you need. Although it may be under investigation by someone else, the issue is ultimately owned by the integration team. Don't lose sight of it.

Common Integration Complaints and Solutions

You're going to have several complaints on that first day, some of which you can resolve and some of which are out of your control. Read all the requests that come through and assign the right person to do the appropriate research. Your coverage is specifically with the middleware ETL tool, so you'll be escalating your tickets back to the source/target systems if the issue lies purely with the data; a field that seemed so right in the source system was actually rife with typos. Only in the new light of day and application is it noticeable.

Here are some of the common complaints you'll receive and how to solve them. This list is not complete but should cover most of the items that will come your way:

- Complaint: "The field is missing."

  - What to Do: Start with looking at the ETL code and confirm that, yes, the field is missing. Open the latest version of the Source-to-Target Mapping and see if the value was on the list for migration/ integration.

Note   Invariably, you'll encounter data stewards who will want to know why a particular field was not transformed the way it should be or why it was omitted when it should have been included. If done right, your STTM will contain notes on why fields were adjusted from their original designation, the data owner who made that request, and who approved it. In all honesty, there is nothing as satisfying as that moment when you recount to the data stewards that *they* were the ones who requested to modify the field in the first place, followed by the reasons why and the exact date.

And, yes, there is always the possibility that the integration team missed a field. In those cases, you'll want to prepare for an emergency update to take place as soon as you get signoff from management (see "Updating Production" later in this chapter).

- Complaint: "The data is transformed incorrectly."

  - What to Do: Again, this is one for review and research. The STTM should have all the details you need in the Transformation Rules field. If you find that, indeed, the actual data does not match with the blueprint, then work with your ETL developers to figure out why and what happened. It could be incorrect code, missed exception logic, or something entirely unexpected that interrupted sequencing during migration. Once you've found the root cause, make the fix on your ETL code and go through the documentation-fix cycle along with testing. Once it's working, redeploy your ETL code and work with teams to update the incorrectly transformed Production data.

- Complaint: "The ETL is broken/didn't run."

    - What to Do: The ETL not running correctly is one we hear a lot from the target data owners who, inundated with tickets, are trying to make sense of why the data from the previous night's run hasn't shown up where they expect it to be. Fortunately, you'll have previous execution logs at your disposal and can either confirm or deny the possibility. If the ETL job failed to execute on schedule, figure out the cause. If it was a minor glitch or due to temporary failure, submit a response ticket to rerun the job on demand or, if preferred, on schedule. If the cause was something more serious, like the ETL triggered an error and ended the job abruptly, then proceed back to the code and, using execution logs and a testing environment, reproduce the issue. Once found, continue in the usual way with updating the documentation and performing the patch in Production.

- Complaint: "I don't have information on what happened, but I know something isn't right with the data."

    - What to Do: "Something not right with the data" is a common complaint as, for most people outside the immediate team, the ETL process is mostly transparent. They don't know about the source, the target, the ETL, or any of the other architectural detail, but only that the records they see don't meet their expectations or memory. Consequently, without conclusive evidence, this is a tough one to debug. Try to get as much information as you can, look into all the possibilities (check the previous ETL execution logs, investigate any additional duplicate errors that may have been reported, ask the source and target data owners if any potential impacts might have caused data issues). You initially may come up empty on a cause, but if it's a legitimate issue, it will crop up again. Hopefully, this time around, you'll have more information with which to work.

The Daily Data Log

One of the best mitigators to identifying data issues ahead of your customers is to create a Daily Data Log, a once-a-day document that takes the lines of logged data from your ETL executions and consolidates it into a simple report that provides summary statistics on the entire repeatable integration. The Daily Data Log includes the process name, the time the first job ran, the time the job ended, the total count of records passed, the total number of errors (if any), and the category of these errors (Business versus Technical and then some; see Chapter 7 for definitions). Sharing this document with your data owners through a wiki, daily email, or reporting application will quickly identify focal points and issues both your team and they might have otherwise missed as well as provide a starting point for continuous improvement within your organization. We'll talk more about continuous improvement in the next section.

Note   Although I recommend building a Daily Data Log via scripts you have at your disposal, there are more professional solutions on the market today. You can review application monitoring systems from various vendors such as Datadog, SmartBear, New Relic, and Atlassian, to name a few. These are worth looking into and provide excellent features that can significantly boost your ability to find and fix problems.

Updating Production

You should do your best to avoid changing your ETL code directly in Production. During our discussion of technical debt (Chapter 7), I recommended that you build a strategy that allows you to provide parameters for changing values rather than hardcoding. But sometimes it's impossible to avoid touching Production—there might be an emergency fix, some crippling piece of code that brings down the database,[3] or some critical requirement that was deemed inconsequential through the chain by everyone except the CEO who now has gotten hold of Production. In that case, you'll have to jump right in. Do it methodically and consistently. I define a strategy I usually employ in Figure 8-2.

---

[3]Paul Morris, Oliver Haslam, RP Staff, Oliver Haslam, and Sameed Khan. 2019. "This Text Message Can Crash, Reboot Any Iphone Instantly | Redmond Pie." *Redmond Pie.* www.redmondpie.com/ this-text-message-can-crash-reboot-any-iphone-instantly/

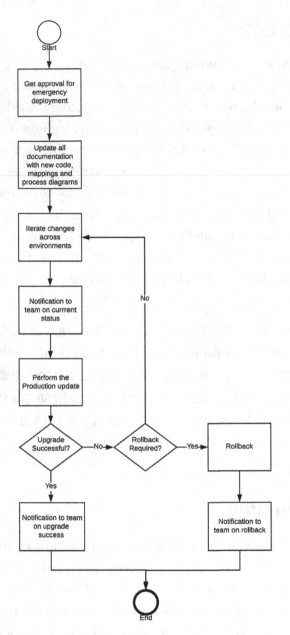

Figure 8-2. *Production Update Flowchart*

Summary of steps:

1. Reach out to your project manager or business stakeholder for approval; open a change management ticket if necessary.

2. Update your project documentation—realign the Source-to-Target mapping, make changes to the Data Migration Process Flow Diagram and details, and communicate with your development team on required changes, making sure you get a realistic LOE.

3. Iterate through your changes, starting with the development environment, testing, deploying to staging, retesting, and finally sharing any prototypes of fixes with those concerned.

4. Following your company's policies, send a notification to the affected teams on the cause, workaround, expected impacts, and downtime of the Production server. Let them know whom to contact in case they encounter issues with the new upgrade.

5. Perform the updates. When completed, send another notification to the affected teams with the latest status as well as whom to contact in case of continued issues. Most importantly, thank them for their patience and support in handling the downtime.

6. If, for whatever reason, you cannot fix the issue, and it is indeed a showstopper for the product, then you may have to roll back Production to the copy immediately before the breakage. Yes, this is the worst-case scenario, and no one wants this option, but it's better than the nightmare scenario where you accidentally wipe out data and cause incalculable harm to your systems.[4]

Week One: Post-deployment

During that first week, you've probably made a few tweaks to your ETL script and maybe a few emergency deployments (let's not hope too many). At this point, the users increasingly are becoming engaged with the new system, and you hear both the pros and cons of the work your team has done. Pay attention to this gossip and take notes. Sure, the system works, but it can always be improved. That's a goal about which we will need to start thinking.

---

[4]For the nightmare scenario, see "Accidentally Destroyed Production Database on First Day of a Job..." 2019. *Reddit*. www.reddit.com/r/cscareerquestions/comments/6ez8ag/accidentally_destroyed_production_database_on/

Planning Your Next Steps

If you're keeping track of your start and end times for each job, you're going to start seeing some common patterns. Perhaps there's a job that runs too slowly at 2:00 a.m. or one that times out under defined thresholds. Your users may not consider these major issues or, at the most, will tolerate them with some grumbling. Although you may be inclined to ignore the problem—if it ain't broke to them, why fix it?—I recommend that you persist in finding a solution. First, just because no one sees it as an issue now doesn't mean it won't be in the future, especially if your source and target systems are going to take on additional loads. Second, the more optimization you can achieve in each load, the better you'll be able to measure your integration consistently without interruption. This optimization is critical in identifying additional opportunities through a productivity concept known as continuous improvement.

Continuous Improvement

Continuous improvement goes by many names: "rapid improvement," Kaizen, and incrementalism,[5] and is a subset of the general process of improvement posited by W. Edwards Deming in the 1950s.[6] In the realm of data integration, we can boil down our definition as "focusing on linear improvement, streamlining work, and reducing irrelevancy through automated, scalable solutions."[7] What this means is that by observing and continuously iterating our ETL streams to accelerate delivery, we will eventually reach a level of maximum productivity. Although achieving total automation would be optimal—the fastest speed with no user intervention whatsoever—we acknowledge that there will always be space for further improvement.

Reaching the next level of productivity is a significant driver for our team and one that should be at the heart of our integration roadmaps (more on that in Chapter 9). For the time being, the easiest way for us to determine what requires improvement is

---

[5]"Related Words—Find Words Related to Another Word." 2019. Relatedwords.org. `https://relatedwords.org/relatedto/continuous%20improvement`

[6]"Continuous Improvement Model—Continual Improvement Tools | ASQ." 2019. Asq.org. `https://asq.org/quality-resources/continuous-improvement`

[7]"What Is Continuous Improvement? | Planview Leankit." 2019. *Planview*. `www.planview.com/resources/articles/what-is-continuous-improvement/`

through the Plan-Do-Check-Act (PDCA) model proposed by Deming and refined by others (see Figure 8-3).[8] We can break down the acronym as follows:

- Plan: Define the problem to be addressed, collect the data, and determine the root cause.

- Do: Develop a solution, and decide on a measurement to ascertain the effectiveness.

- Check: Confirm the results through before-and-after data comparisons.

- Act: Document the results, let others know about process changes, and recommend for them to address the problems.

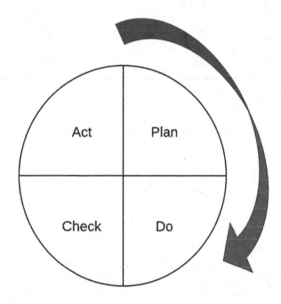

Figure 8-3. *PDCA Model*

Keep in mind that our focus for this continuous improvement stays primarily within our domain, namely, the ETL process. It is tempting for us to suggest that we innovate the source and target side of the house, especially if we find improvements needed in that area. Although feedback to these teams is encouraged, trying to include these systems as part of your team's ETL project can be viewed as meddling. It is better to get the source and target teams to agree with your assessment rather than usurping systems that are others' responsibility.

---

[8]"What Is PDCA (Plan-Do-Check-Act)?—Definition from Whatis.Com." 2019. *Whatis.com.* https://whatis.techtarget.com/definition/PDCA-plan-do-check-act

With this introduction, we can look at a simple PDCA example. Let's say that after the first week of execution, you analyze your log files for the five jobs you run each evening. Using your reporting tool, you graph your execution times in seconds (see Table 8-1 and the corresponding line graph in Figure 8-4).

Table 8-1. *Execution Times (sec.) of Jobs per Day*

JobName	Monday	Tuesday	Wednesday	Thursday	Friday	Saturday	Sunday
Job 1	30	29	28	30	33	28	28
Job 2	22	24	24	21	21	22	24
Job 3	18	18	18	18	17	19	18
Job 4	67	52	79	87	47	30	30
Job 5	32	35	35	35	33	27	35

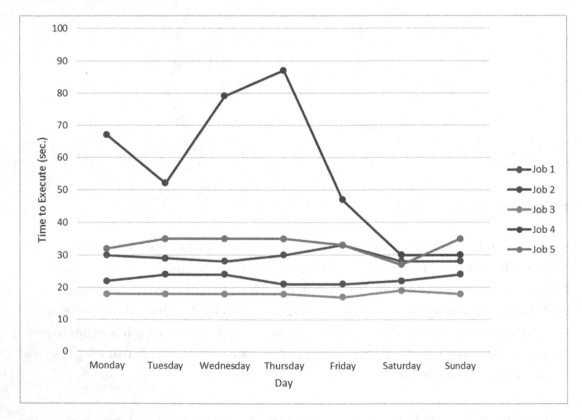

Figure 8-4. *Job Execution Day by Time (s)*

By looking at the day-over-day variability, we can see there's something unusual with Job 4. It seems like its timing from start to finish is much higher than the other jobs on our list. Of course, timing is only one factor to consider, and there may be other issues to explore. But as a first pass, a suitable candidate for improvement is with Job 4 and its above-average timing.

With this observation in place, you're now ready to start your PDCA analysis:

- Plan: Figure out what is causing Job 4 to have this variability. To do this, set up additional timers in your code and track across the next several days. Is this issue consistent or just a bump in the road due to some unrelated issue like a network delay? Are there any particular data points that may be tying up the system or any part of the code that seems to take longer than others?

To show our Plan step in action, let's look at Job 4 execution times over a week. We'll use a bar chart to see our pattern (see Figure 8-5).

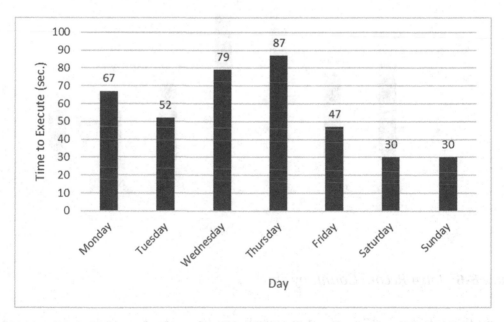

Figure 8-5. *Job 4 Execution Day by Time (s)*

We can interpret from the chart that Monday, Wednesday, and Thursday took a longer time to execute and that the scores seem to have a high amount of variability day over day. For those of you into statistics, our average over the week is 56 seconds, with a standard deviation of 22.58. In other words, we could expect during that initial week to have an execution ranging from 10.8 seconds up to 101.1 seconds about 95% of the time. This range is hugely unpredictable and makes it difficult for us to estimate our execution time. It could be a big problem as well if our data connection forces a timeout due to inactivity.

During your analysis of the log files, you look at as many metrics as you can. For example, you can plot the number of records that were retrieved. Lo and behold, you find that these record counts were much higher on Monday, Wednesday, and Thursday than the other four days (see Table 8-2 and the corresponding graph of Figure 8-6).

Table 8-2. *Job 4 Record Counts by Day*

JobName	Monday	Tuesday	Wednesday	Thursday	Friday	Saturday	Sunday
Job 4	52,175	40,508	61,541	67,773	36,613	23,370	23,370

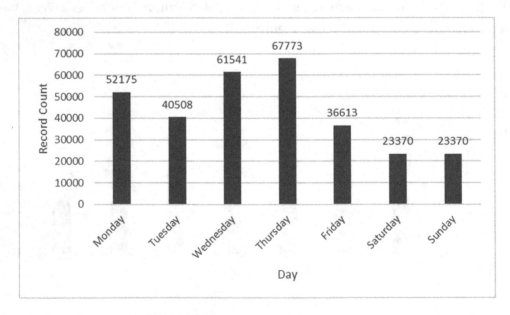

Figure 8-6. *Job 4 Record Counts by Day*

Isn't that interesting? The count of records per day seems to correlate almost with the throughput in seconds per day. That is, the higher the record count, the longer the job takes to execute. Perhaps that's the issue?

- Do: For the Do phase, you'll think about your problem statement and the options for solving it. We'll start with the theory that higher record counts are leading to greater throughput (makes sense, right?).

What value are we going to use to measure this? Would we want to test performance over time, a lower record count, or something else? Really, it's up to you, as this is only testing your hypothesis. If you don't get the results you want, you can always try the different approaches you have in mind.

You want to come up with a shortlist of solutions, and you should pick your best option as the one that (a) seems the most likely and (b) is the easiest to implement. For example, you could increase the speed of throughput in several ways, like activating parallel processing (i.e., pulling back more records from the database). Or you could limit the count of records retrieved with some SQL language and then execute the job multiple times instead of just once (for example, SELECT LIMIT keyword and OFFSET if you're using certain types of databases).[9]

After weighing the pros and cons and talking with your developers on the likelihood and ease of implementation, the team decides that the second option with LIMIT/OFFSET is the best design because it would take longer to enable the parallel processing feature and there's less risk to the overall job—you don't want to fix one issue only to create another. Keep in mind once again that if it doesn't work, you can always choose your plan B, C, or D (whatever letter suits you).

Note   When designing your solutions, you're going to want to have a precise measurement in mind. For instance, if we're trying to limit the records returned, you don't want to make it too high as it could grind your system to a halt, but you also don't want to be too conservative that you have 15 separate executions carrying only 5000 records. Think of it like being Goldilocks, but with data instead of porridge and your ETL code instead of bears. Pick a target value and stick with it.

We've talked it over and would like each execution to take about 30 seconds. Sure, we'll launch the job multiple times a day, but we'll have predictability instead of variability; that's where we want our continuous improvement to take us.

- Check: Once you've made the updates to your code, you're ready to test in your Staging environment. Create data that matches what you might typically receive and then execute and replot.

---

[9]"SQL: SELECT LIMIT Statement." 2019. Techonthenet.com. www.techonthenet.com/sql/select_limit.php

We've got a good data generator and can create fake data that matches the counts we received that first week. If you don't have a good data generator, check out two online apps Mockaroo (*https://www.mockaroo.com/*)[10] and Generate Data (*http://www. generatedata.com/*).[11] These tools allow you to save data in several formats and even automate scripts if you have the technical know-how.

To review our strategy: Rather than running our job just once a day, we now will run multiple times a day with 25,000 records each. Table 8-3 shows the breakdown of test record counts executed in parallel.

Table 8-3. *Test Record Counts Executed in Parallel*

JobName	Test Day 1	Test Day 2	Test Day 3	Test Day 4	Test Day 5	Test Day 6	Test Day 7
Job 4 #1	25,000	25,000	25,000	25,000	25,000	23,370	23,370
Job 4 #2	25,000	15,508	25,000	25,000	11,613		
Job 4 #3	2,175		11,541	17,773			
TOTAL	52,175	40,508	61,541	67,773	36,613	23,370	23,370

In this simulated dataset, you'll notice three modifications. First, we're not tracking days, but rather test executions. This approach accelerates our time to deliver. Second, the cumulative total of jobs we run per "day" is equal to our original record count. This technique provides like-for-like comparisons. Third, the execution will not need to run if we use up our test records before reaching the 25,000 record limit. For example, Test Day 2 only had 40,508 records. The first execution consists of 25,000, and the second is equal to the remaining 40,508 – 25,000 = 15,508. There's no need for a third execution.

We've picked 25,000 because that seems like a good starting point—not too much and also not too little. Plus, it looks like our Saturday and Sunday jobs in our original execution (Figure 8-5) took about 30 seconds to run, and that meets our target goal.

Displaying this dataset as a stacked bar chart reveals the same shape as previously graphed (see Figure 8-7).

---

[10]"Mockaroo—Random Data Generator and API Mocking Tool | JSON/CSV/SQL/Excel." 2019. Mockaroo.com. www.mockaroo.com/

[11]"Generatedata.Com." 2019. *Generatedata.com*. www.generatedata.com/

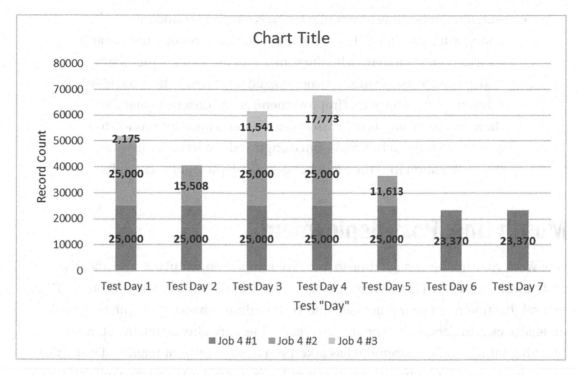

Figure 8-7. *Cumulative Record Count by Test Day*

To confirm the processing speed, we gather each execution time from our log files (see Table 8-4).

Table 8-4. *Test Record Times (sec.) Executed in Parallel*

JobName	Test Day 1	Test Day 2	Test Day 3	Test Day 4	Test Day 5	Test Day 6	Test Day 7
Job 4 #1	30	29	28	30	33	28	28
Job 4 #2	31	20	29	28	18		
Job 4 #3	7		18	24			

Now, our sets of 25,000 records per execution appear to be much more stable. If we were to summarize that first job run, we would average 29.43 records with a standard deviation (variability) of 1.81. That is, 95% of the time during these test days, we will expect to have execution times between 25.80 and 33.05. That measurement is more constained than our original set and allows us to have a fair amount of predictability on our performance going forward.

- Act: Remember, this is only one analysis, and no production changes have been implemented. But you have a lot of numbers and measurements to share with the source and target team members and guidance for the next process upgrade. Let them know the effort it will take to perform this improvement, get a consensus that the direction you chose is the correct one (is 30 seconds for this job too short? Is it too much?), and—once approved—start revising your documentation with the new changes and deployment schedule.

Month One: Post-deployment

One week may not be enough time to trace your improvement plans, and after the first month, the system is humming along, you've identified some work through PDCA that might streamline your processes, and you continue a backlog of updates based on feedback and personal observations. Stakeholders are already talking about the "next big thing," and management has asked you to position your team to discuss the future migrations and integrations. At this point, you may be asking yourself, "Where is this going? What's my next step?" The answer is a nondefinitive "many places." You've reached the point where you have to decide on whether you keep the status quo by maintaining help desk support and supporting the occasional upgrade or if it's time to push forward and expand your organization's level of data and governance. For that, we'll need to discuss the Data Management Maturity (DMM) model.

The Data Management Maturity (DMM) Model

The DMM model is a process improvement and capability maturity framework for an organization's management of data assets and related activities.[12] It covers the best practices across five levels of functional capability and maturity: Data Management Strategy, Data Quality, Data Operations, Platform and Architecture, and Data

---

[12]"What Is the Data Management Maturity (DMM) Model?" 2019. *CMMI Institute Help Center.* https://cmmiinstitute.zendesk.com/hc/en-us/articles/216335388-What-is-the-Data-Management-Maturity-DMM-model-

Governance (DG). Supporting processes such as Measurement and Analysis, Risk Management, and Configuration Management are also part of the framework, forming a complete strategy (see Figure 8-8).

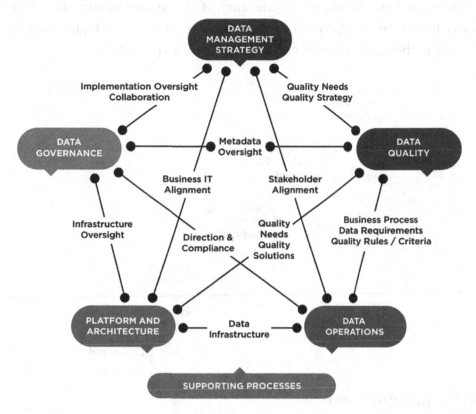

Figure 8-8. Data Maturity Model Categories—From Data Management Maturity (DMM) Model At-A-Glance[13]

By enabling these practices, teams can benchmark their capabilities, identify the data strengths and technological gaps, and leverage their data assets to improve their overall business performance.[14] More importantly, the DMM model is designed in such a way that it can be used to not only assess the current management capabilities but also to build a customized roadmap for future enterprise data enhancements.

[13]2019. Cmmiinstitute.com. https://cmmiinstitute.com/getattachment/cb35800b-720f-4afe-93bf-86ccefb1fb17/attachment.aspx

[14]"CMMI Institute—Data Management Maturity (DMM)—Lifetime License." 2019. Cmmiinstitute. com. https://cmmiinstitute.com/store/data-management-maturity-(dmm)-(1)

Although there are many paths we can take in following the DMM model, the question is how we can leverage it to help us maintain and expand on our integration team. The DMM (which is available for a cost from *https://cmminstitute.com/dmm*) contains a complete set of processes under each of the categories; and each of these processes can, in turn, break down into maturity levels. That is, the higher the level, the more "capable" the organization is concerning their data practice.

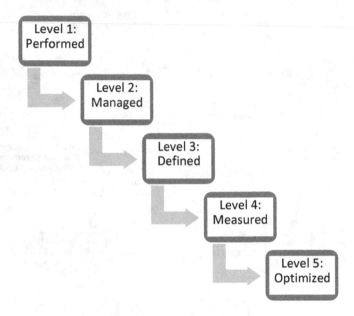

Figure 8-9. *Maturity Levels*

In Figure 8-9, I've illustrated the maturity levels going from least adept to most. The idea is for you to examine each of your practices and to see where you fit in this scale. A brief list of each level with the corresponding definition follows:

- Level 1: Performed

- At this level, formal processes are minimal, and repair takes precedence over prevention. If you've ever been on a team engaged in technical firefighting, this is it. Solutions are improvised at the moment rather than standardized, and there is no consistency in best practice for issue resolution.

- Level 2: Managed

  Processes are in place and planned against the policy, with
  the organization agreeing that managing data is a critical
  infrastructure asset. Systems are monitored to ensure that teams
  adhere to the process, but it is not globally standard. This maturity
  level applies primarily to the single or multiple departments but
  does not encompass the enterprise.

- Level 3: Defined

  At the Defined level, a set of standard processes and
  accompanying guidelines have been adopted by the organization
  and must be consistently followed by all teams. Data is treated at
  the organizational level as critical for performance success.

- Level 4: Measured

  Process metrics are highlighted at this level, and data is treated as
  a source of competitive advantage through the use of statistical
  techniques like forecasting, prediction, and analysis.

- Level 5: Optimized

  At this level, the process metrics taken from Level 4 are used
  to identify new improvement opportunities. The data teams
  are regarded as a leader in their data space, and best practices
  are shared across the industry through conferences, meetups,
  and similar events (refer to Chapter 9). Data is not just viewed
  as critical for performance success but is seen as an absolute
  necessity for surviving in a competitive market.

With the foundations of the DMM categories and subjective ability to assess the
capability maturity level of your team and enterprise, you can start thinking about the
direction you want to go after dipping your toe in the waters of your first integrations.
With the monitoring metrics described in this chapter, you will already be striving for
Level 4 (provided you use metrics like log reports), but there is generally much more of
your silos that you can examine. Do you have Level 1 integration areas that need more
data processes defined? Can these best practices be extended across the organization?
Can you automate many of these processes to the point where data analytics can help
guide you in your next steps? Organizations have a patchwork of data layers, and each one

of them can stimulate ideas for the next step. That is your primary purpose of monitoring following the first month post-deployment—determine your current level of data maturity, decide where you want that level to be, and use the existing analytic data at your disposal—what else requires improvement? Then think about how you will get it done.

Caution   Although most organization leaders have a realistic approach to their maturity model, now and then, you'll run into one with a big, hairy audacious goal (BHAG). You may hear something like "We want to migrate the data, build policy and procedures, use statistics, and become the market leader as quickly as we can. When can you have this done?" While being ambitious has its perks,[15] I would recommend setting the appropriate expectations right from the outset; just one integration project can take time, effort, and more than enough skilled resources. Expanding this model enterprise-wide before the other parts of the organization are ready will lead to disappointment, financial setbacks, and a slew of other frustrations. We'll talk more about getting upper management on board with your team in the next chapter.

Year One: Post-deployment

After a year, you have chosen to fully invest in your data integration system with a few more significant projects under your belt, have documented best practices and policies, have established an on-demand monitoring system, and have a general roadmap for getting close to (or at) DMM Levels 4 and 5.

As your projects expand to other departments, you will notice commonalities among the sourced datasets they provide. For example, the staff in these departments collect their separate versions of accounts, customers, products, and suppliers. Unbeknownst to them, other teams store similar information, perhaps with only a different format or spelling. It is quite common to find that you have three tables among three departments, each containing a variation of the same customer. One table contains last name, first name, middle name, email, and fax; the second contains full name, address, and email; the third contains full name, phone number, email, and age (see Figure 8-10).

---

[15]Harnish, Verne. 2019. "BHAG—Why the Most Successful Companies Set Ambitious, Long-Term Goals & Why Yours Should Too." Blog.growthinstitute.com. https://blog.growthinstitute.com/scale-up-blueprint/bhag-big-hairy-audacious-goal

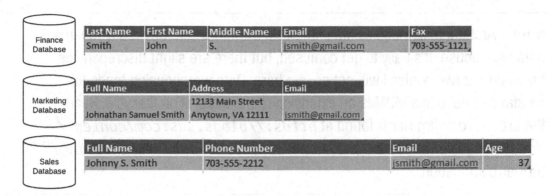

Figure 8-10. *Common CUSTOMER Among Three Separate Databases*

Only through exploration, profiling, and analysis will these commonalities become clear. And when this clarification arrives, you may want to about ways to integrate these separate-but-equal records into a single point of reference. That leads us to the next step in our integration journey, linking critical data into a system known as Master Data Management (MDM).

MDM

As its end goal, an MDM system should be able to consolidate data from multiple system sources into a single view that can then be further retrieved and refined by data teams. For example, if we chose to integrate our distinct customer databases from Figure 8-10 into a single MDM repository table, we could track the complete set of fields (First Name, Last Name, Middle Name, Nicknames, Address, Email, Phone Number, Fax, and Age) (see Figure 8-11).

First Name	Last Name	Middle Name	Nicknames	Address	Email	Phone Number	Fax Number	Age
Johnathan	Smith	Samuel	John, Johnny	12133 Main Street Anytown, VA 12111	jsmith@gmail.com	703-555-2212	703-555-1121	37

Figure 8-11. *Common CUSTOMER MDM View*

> **Note**   Architects sometimes state an MDM system when they really mean a data warehouse. It's easy to get confused, but there are slight discrepancies between the two, which I will not go into here. Data warehousing tends to be standalone, while MDM is an extension of the integration lifecycle. Read the article from Jim Harris found at *https://blogs.sas.com/content/ datamanagement/2017/04/27/mdm-different-data-warehousing/*[16] for further clarification.

Building an MDM can be challenging and spark contention among teams,[17] but the benefits of reuse and standardization can significantly increase response speeds, provide more flexible reporting, and improve data quality. Customizable MDM tools from vendors such as IBM[18] and Dell Boomi[19] offer a single view of the data across the enterprise and may be worth looking into if you want to stand up a solution in a relatively short amount of time and with minimum coding effort.

Summary

In this chapter, we have discussed the post-deployment operation of monitoring and leveraging your log results to ensure a smooth transition into your next activities. Whether you are fixing the existing issues in the short-term days and weeks ahead or continuously improving your process across months and years, your team will always be seeking out ways to minimize data errors, reduce downtime, and further the understanding of where the team should be going next.

In the next chapter, we'll discuss how to spread the word and get the rest of the enterprise involved in your efforts.

---

[16]Harris, Jim. 2019. "How Is MDM Different from Data Warehousing?" *The Data Roundtable*. https://blogs.sas.com/content/datamanagement/2017/04/27/ mdm-different-data-warehousing/

[17]"What Is Master Data Management (MDM) and Why Is It Important?" 2019. *Searchdatamanagement*. https://searchdatamanagement.techtarget.com/definition/ master-data-management

[18]"Master Data Management." 2019. Ibm.com. www.ibm.com/analytics/ master-data-management

[19]"Master Data Hub Tools—MDM Solutions | Boomi." 2019. *Boomi*. https://boomi.com/ platform/master-data-hub/

CHAPTER 9

Marketing Your Team

Coming together is a beginning, staying together is progress, and working together is success.

—Henry Ford[1]

Introduction

At this point in our journey, the integration team has set up best practices and guidelines, deployed several projects, and established monitoring and analytics systems and has some direction for creating and improving future integration projects. We've hit a crossroads where we need to expand our practice, and there's one final thing you'll need to consider: enterprise participation.

I mentioned much earlier in this book that you can have the best bells and whistles on a software application, but if the data within that application is incorrect, then none of those features matter. Bad input will equal bad output. To continue that thought, you can have the best integration system in the world, but if no one uses it, then it serves no purpose. Data does not exist for data's sake. It is used to answer analytic questions, make better predictions, and discover previously unforeseen patterns. If the audience posing these statements is absent, then you have no inertia to move forward, no matter how optimal the process or the data may be.

Lack of user support may not entirely rest on you. The process itself may have been designed with the best intentions in mind, but your advertisement strategy hasn't worked, or it may not have the needed reputation, or users might misunderstand its purpose. On the other hand, the process actually may be broken, in which case

---

[1]"31 Collaboration Quotes to Ignite Successful Teamwork." 2019. *Bit Blog.* `https://blog.bit.ai/teamwork-collaboration-quotes/`

© Jarrett Goldfedder 2020
J. Goldfedder, *Building a Data Integration Team,* https://doi.org/10.1007/978-1-4842-5653-4_9

I encourage you to go back to the previous chapters and reread steps for iterating on your existing design and bringing it back into alignment with the enterprise vision. In any case, don't sell yourself short. Having the ability to grow the integration platform is critical to reaching the next level of development.

In this chapter, I'll cover some of the essential aspects of marketing the work you've done and positioning your team for successful growth. We'll discuss how to address leadership, educating your users, promoting through external events, building a roadmap for the future, and defining your rules with a Data Governance Office. By the end of this chapter, you should be in an excellent position to start reaching out to end users and, at the very least, to have fresh ideas for inspiring a team who is hungry for growth.

Addressing Leadership

You may be curious why, after having gone through each step to build your team and product, you lost the support that initially propelled you forward. After all, there was a problem to solve, and you formed a well-documented system that established stakeholder support with a rollout met with great fanfare. Why, then, after the post-deployment stage, did all that goodwill dry up? Couldn't they see the value that the integration effort provided? Isn't it evident that the continued development of these processes will benefit the organization as a whole?

Well, no, not exactly. There are many reasons why projects fail to gain additional support. One of the most important ones we'll discuss is a lack of buy-in from executives—that is, the ones who drive the vision forward and hold the purse strings for the budget. From personal experience, I have observed that if the C-level management (CIO, CEO, CFO) does not believe that your integrations and automation approach will earn value for the company, then it will be difficult, if not impossible, to garner support from the people who report up to them. It just isn't on the radar.

The number one secret to make your team grow, then, is to get the leadership on board with your effort, not just for the odd one-off "this would be nice" project, but at the "we need to do this or else" size commitment. Thus, rather than stressing the speed and accuracy for a department that you've delivered in the past, it's time to drive home the benefits for the entire enterprise. How do integrations impact the bottom line? What matters to your leaders? According to blogger Mike Raia, selling the workflow automation might involve the following topics:[2]

- Provide More Data Analysis and Less Non-value Work: Less administrative effort will be needed as your leaders will no longer fumble to find emails and forms and instead can focus on data analysis. Records are just a data click away, and the intradepartmental communication will be more consistent and effective.

- Shift from Application Building to Value Creation: Rather than spending time building and supporting siloed data applications, departments will have a common platform that they can then share with customers. Thus, if designed that way, the data that the customer in China sees is the same as the data in Germany, the United States, France, so on and so forth. One product name change could cascade across the different enterprise systems in near-real time, allowing the organization to pass information as a unified structure.

- Remediate Security Threats: Because your integration systems are monitored under one common umbrella, your process can incorporate a consistent response and predictable defense to identified security threats. You will have integration backups, logged reports, and auditing capabilities to further protect your critical data.

- Improve Data Compliance: Policies and procedures are part of the built-in business rules in your transformations. The integration systems can be a part of a compliance workflow model, alerting if there are any outliers to internal or external regulation breaches. If done correctly, data compliance becomes standardized, enforceable, and auditable, protecting companies from major legal issues.

---

[2]"Why the C-Level Loves Business Process Automation." 2019. *Workflow Management Software by Integrify*. www.integrify.com/blog/posts/why-the-c-level-loves-business-process-automation/

- Standardize Revenue: One of the prime targets for an integration system are the various payment systems associated with customer revenue and retention. With the right architecture, profitability data could be exported to a centralized capture area. Thus, rather than expending time and resources reaching across various platforms, determining a company's bottom line could be a matter of aggregating the numbers from just a few target locations.

- Increase Employee Satisfaction and Raise Company Culture: If the preceding benefits are realized, then life becomes sweeter for everyone: the employees can focus on the day-to-day activities rather than the minutiae of operations, the organization becomes more transparent in terms of compliance and errors, and improved analysis of data will spark the creative edge that companies require to be successful. In short, having a top-shelf integration process could mean massive growth which, in turn, would lead to an improved bottom line, a stellar reputation, and a penchant for flexibility, all of which customers highly admire in today's competitive business culture.

Of course, acquiring management support is just one factor in a list of many for why one team will succeed and another one might die on the vine.[3] Still, if you do everything right and always find yourself unable to gain a wider audience with more projects, it may be time for you to focus on reaching out to management. By taking the risk, you have everything to gain.

Educating Others

It may not be easy to get that audience with the Chief Executive Officer, Chief Information Officer, or Chief Financial Officer. That's okay: in time, they'll come around, and when they do, you'll be ready with a list of your marketing points. Still, it's essential to run with Plan B and to get the word out about the services and benefits that you and your team provide to the organization at large. This strategy will require you to reach out to

---

[3]Lehtonen, Karri. 2019. "10 Reasons Why Integration Projects Fail." Youredi.com. www.youredi.com/blog/10-reasons-why-integration-projects-fail

anyone who has interest but to do so in a professional way without having to resort to "hallway ambushes" or sales pitches. The approach you'll want to establish is training others on what the team does, how they do it, and why. While these types of discussions can often take place in a formal classroom, there are other effective ways to get the point across that do not require face-to-face formality. Let's discuss some of these techniques.

Internal Education

Most of the time, you'll want to disseminate information only to others within your organization. In this case, your audience will be your coworkers. Unless you're doing some knowledge sharing that impacts the industry, the details you provide will be kept in-house through formal seminars, workshops, online training, or lunch and learns.

Formal Seminars

When we discuss "teaching," this is probably the first method of communication that comes to mind. A seminar is "a commercial program where attendees are given information or training about a specific topic."[4] Generally, we think of a teacher-student setup in which one person speaks to a group of people in a classroom or conference room for a set duration (see Figure 9-1).

Traditionally, seminars are the best medium for providing information, but communication is one way from the presenter; responses from the participants are low except during the occasional Q&A. When it comes to training others on integration, a seminar can be helpful if you merely want to present information about the work you've done, the direction you're heading, and the impact that the projects have made. Because integrations get technical very quickly, especially when presenting technical details, the lack of active participation can take its toll on your audience, so be aware of the energy level. We probably all have attended discussions that were scheduled on a Friday afternoon or right before a major holiday. Although the topic may have interested us initially, the seminar itself may not have had any value, and we probably could have gotten the same information through some other method.

---

[4]"What You Need to Know About Seminar Planning." 2019. *The Balance Small Business.* www.thebalancesmb.com/what-is-a-seminar-1223636

Figure 9-1. *Formal Seminar*

Workshops

A workshop is similar to a seminar in that it has an information component to it, but it is more experiential in that workshops involve participants in the learning process by utilizing small and large group discussions, activities and exercises, and ways to practice applying the presented concepts (see Figure 9-2).[5] The workshop leaders (known as facilitators) keep everyone on track and expect all attendees to contribute.

Because migrations and integrations strongly depend on design models and transformation comparisons, a workshop is a great way to learn the basics. By having students walk through the step-by-step process involved with software development, similar to the path we've taken in this book, you can build enthusiasm for the work that exists as well as gain new customers for your cause. But workshops are not for everyone. Some people may feel obliged to attend because their managers recommended it. Others may be less technically savvy than their counterparts or, unbelievable as it may sound, might not have any interest in the fields of integration. Those people would be better off avoiding the workshop as it would only cause more confusion or be detrimental in building group unity. I am confident that no one wants that.

---

[5]"Seminars vs. Workshops." 2019. *Speakernetnews.com*. www.speakernetnews.com/post/ seminarworkshop.html

Figure 9-2. *Workshops*[6]

Online Training

Online training is a teaching program available in the form of software that teaches learners through informal questionnaires; fill-in-the-blank, multiple-choice, and true/false tests; and demonstrations. Online training moves from the physical classroom to the virtual one and can be live, as with a webinar, or recorded for on-demand viewing (see Figure 9-3). The variety of online delivery can vary, usually structured as video, audio, animation, or a combination of methods.[7]

Online training has several advantages over formal seminars: such classes can be run anytime and anywhere computers or mobile devices are found, are usually cheaper, require less of an overall time investment, and have demonstrated higher long-term student retention.[8] From the standpoint of the instructor—the role your team will play—the learning material you create can be more thorough in an online training course, allowing hours of instruction that cover many technical details or, if just an overview is needed, creating a standard slide presentation on the basic outline of your projects.

---

[6]"Workshop Clipart PNG and Cliparts for Free Download—Clipart Collection." 2019. *Boxtutor.com*. http://boxtutor.com/clip-art/workshop-clipart.html

[7]"What Is Online Training? | Eztalks." 2019. *Eztalks.com*. www.eztalks.com/training/what-is-online-training.html

[8]"5 Reasons Why Online Learning Is More Effective." 2019. *Dexway*. www.dexway.com/5-reasons-why-online-learning-is-more-effective/

Figure 9-3. *Online Training*[9]

Lunch and Learns

One of the better ways to get your point across but in a more informal manner is through a lunch and learn, typically a session where a team shares their skills and expertise with others (see Figure 9-4). So named because it often takes place at lunch, the sessions last between 30 and 45 minutes and could be a one-off meeting or delivered as a series of courses.[10]

A lunch and learn has several advantages over the previous methods described. Because it takes place in a social atmosphere, these group meetings encourage teamwork and cooperation, breaking down silos among teams that generally might be guarded during more formal presentations. I remember one particular session where a manager, notoriously famous for refusing to commit resources outside of his group, was so intrigued by the migration team's "Where Are We Now" lunch and learn that he scheduled a more formal follow-up meeting with his lead developers the following week. A great partnership developed from that first session, and future lunch and learns among his peers became a routine practice.

Lunch and learns do have their negatives as well, especially if your team members are remote and cannot be physically in the room. With the use of conferencing tools such

---

[9]Terpakai, Kami. 2019. "Kami Membeli Laptop Terpakai/Used, KL N9 SELANGOR, Nilai (2019)." *Globalnpo.org.* www.globalnpo.org/MY/Nilai/632721646897907/Kami-Membeli-Laptop-Terpakai-Used

[10]"How to Run Successful Lunch and Learn Events: Learning While You Eat." 2019. *Mindtools.com.* www.mindtools.com/pages/article/lunch-and-learn.htm

as Webex (*https://www.webex.com/*), Join.me (*https://www.join.me/*), or Google Hangouts (*https://hangouts.google.com/*), you can minimize some of these drawbacks, but I always experience the feeling that I might miss something as opposed to the face-to-face experience and focus. Be mindful of others when inviting your audience: lunch and learns should be voluntary and relaxed, a knowledge sharing session among interested parties rather than a mandatory meeting. Finally, make sure that the food options are well known, not just the dietary restrictions of your participants, which is essential, but also the cost of the lunch if not on the company's budget. Don't forget to include that tidbit in your calendar invite: I've been to sessions where the leaders expected us to bring individual meals but forgot to tell the participants. There are few things more disappointing than being hungry and realizing you are now in a 45-minute meeting with no food options. In these scenarios, the proverb "no such thing as a free lunch" becomes remarkably accurate.[11]

Figure 9-4. *Lunch and Learn*[12]

Whatever internal training method you choose, you'll want your audience to have specific takeaways and ideas for the next steps. At a broad level, you should provide an understanding of the work that the integration team has accomplished, the benefits

[11]Martin, Gary. 2019. "'There's No Such Thing as a Free Lunch'—the Meaning and Origin of This Phrase." *Phrasefinder*. www.phrases.org.uk/meanings/tanstaafl.html

[12]2019. *Fabricmate.Com.* https://fabricmate.com/wp-content/uploads/2015/05/Lunch-Learn-Image-01-Custom.png

this work has produced over time, and the impact that future work will have for the enterprise and specific departments. Most importantly, you'll want to stress what you need to achieve the next steps. These steps can be through monetary support such as funding an effort, physical participation with resources or systems, or even just helping teams connect the dots to see the bigger picture and know where your team fits in the larger schema.

External Education

At the same time that you are promoting your team, products, and processes in-house, you'll want to reach outside your organization as well. One of the best reasons for doing that is promotion: your team is doing some great work, and letting others in the industry know this is the best case for wanting to purchase or partner with your organization. It also improves team morale—when workers see how their work makes a difference to others both in and out of their respective workgroups, both job satisfaction and productivity significantly improve.[13] Thus, attending activities off the job such as meetups, networking events, and conferences can have a long-term influence on increasing the growth of your team.

External education is not for everyone, however. There are times when this type of promotion should be minimized or even avoided. For example, you may not have enough internal buy-in to ensure outside success. Or you may mistrust that your competitors will copy the proprietary ideas you present.[14] For any of these situations, reach out to your legal department and policymakers before committing your teammates to speak on any topics.

For now, we'll go with the understanding that your team has performed some significant accomplishments, is getting the name across the enterprise, and has now decided to share with the industry at large. How should you start?

---

[13]"Making a Difference at Work." 2019. *Psychology Today.* www.psychologytoday.com/us/articles/200407/making-difference-work

[14]Kritti B., Aman Rawat, Meha A., Kopal C., Yatti Soni, and Bhumika K. 2019. "My Advice to the World's Entrepreneurs: Copy and Steal—the Silicon Valley Way." *Inc42 Media.* https://inc42.com/resources/my-advice-to-the-worlds-entrepreneurs-copy-and-steal-the-silicon-valley-way/

Meetups

Probably the best way to begin is by finding people who are interested in the same topics as you. Merriam-Webster defines a "meetup" as "an informal meeting or gathering."[15] In the early 2000s, the word became synonymous with a free social network web site, Meetup.com, that enables users to organize meetings in a local area.[16] Meetup.com is an excellent resource for meeting new people, practicing a language, teaching a class, or marketing a brand. The groups you choose to follow will cover just about any topic out there. Still, if you can't find what you want, you can always start a new group with only a few clicks.

JOINING MEETUP.COM.

- Go to "Meetup.com" and click the "Log in" link (see Figure 9-5). There are multiple ways to sign up through Facebook, Google, or email. Once verified, you can begin exploring your way through the groups and events that are available in your area.

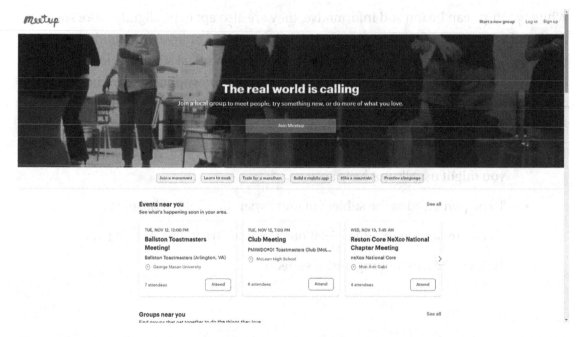

Figure 9-5. *Meetup.com Home Page*

---

[15]"Definition of MEETUP." 2019. *Merriam-Webster.Com.* www.merriam-webster.com/dictionary/meetup

[16]"Meetup: What Is Meetup?" 2019. *Gcfglobal.org.* https://edu.gcfglobal.org/en/meetup/what-is-meetup/1/

- For our current discussion, you'll want to use data-savvy search words like "migration," "integration," "analytics," or "reporting." If none of these appear as a result, then you may want to consider organizing the event by clicking the "Start a new group" link and answering the steps that follow.

Caution   Meetups are a lot of fun and a great way to meet people with similar interests. Be careful, though. Initially, I applied to more than a dozen topics surrounding data integration, warehousing, and reporting, expecting that I would be able to socialize in all of them. As it turned out, being spread too thin was just as bad as not having enough choices. I would recommend you decide your priorities and the goal of your meetup approach and then go all out to make it happen.

Networking Event

While meetups can be fun and informative, they are also apt to be slightly more social than professional networking events in which the goals are more about building business relationships and trust and not necessarily boosting your social status, swapping business cards, or finding the next big event in town.[17] Professional networking, in this case, is something that can involve lifelong relationships. According to a post by author Anders Ostlund,[18] networking has many benefits:

- To gain knowledge and information on a product or service to which you might usually not have access

- To be perceived as the subject matter expert in a field of business

- To create new professional relationships and strengthen existing ones

- To increase trust among business peers

---

[17]"The Difference Between Networking and Making Friends." 2019. *The Muse*. www.themuse.com/advice/the-difference-between-networking-and-making-friends

[18]Ostlund, Anders. 2019. "What Is Professional Networking and Why Is It Important?—Fryday™." *Fryday.net*. www.fryday.net/blog/post/what-is-professional-networking-and-why-is-it-important-6/

- To make sure that people know who you are, what you do, how you do it, and what you want to achieve by doing it

- To establish you and your teams as an authority

Professional networking feeds upon itself. You may make an effective presentation to your networking group, and one of those members may, in turn, ask you to speak to another group about that topic. This domino effect can lead to more followers and access to more events and may elevate your team as the "go-to" group when it comes to building and maintaining migrations. The many skills you develop from this activity—mastering small talk, sharing content, creating relationships—can last with you across your career and help enhance your teams' brand in the marketplace.

Events come in all shapes and sizes, ranging from trade fairs to after-work happy hours to conferences (which we'll discuss next). The best way to get started is to use your favorite search engine and type the phrase "professional networking events in my area." You'll most likely get enough results to keep you busy for a while.

Although professional networking can favor the extroverts, if you are shy or uncomfortable about meeting new people, show up anyway. At some point, the conversation is likely to drift into your territory, and it is there that you'll be able to shine or, at the very least, impart some knowledge about your team and what they do.

Conferences

Conferences are perhaps the most significant networking events in an industry with most of the benefits that professional networking entails. However, these types of gatherings often are much larger and complex than local events, occur less frequently, and involve speakers, sponsors, and other representatives who sell products, educate, and provide technological insight. The conferences may last a few days or up to a week. Like all good networking events, its purpose is to create enthusiasm and inspiration and enable the attendee to feel much wiser at the end of the sessions.

For all its glitz, glamour, and good food, the main reason people attend conferences is the same as other networking events except that the outreach is much more extensive.[19] One of the most significant events in North America is Salesforce's annual

---

[19]"Why Do People Attend Conferences? 5 Key Reasons." 2019. *Curtis & Coulter*. https://curtiscoulter.com/why-do-people-attend-conferences-5-key-reasons-for-attendees-and-event-organizers/

Dreamforce conference, with more than 170,000 participants.[20] Against those types of numbers, you potentially would be associating with people from all over the world and in all professions. Conferences are exciting and a great way to engage yourself in the industry. If planned right, the takeaways will work wonders for guiding your integration team and gaining momentum for the next steps.

Of course, many people go to conferences with no clear strategy or intention. Yes, there can be socializing, and there can be taking a break from work. If those are your goals, then that's fine. But for actual growth, what you want to do is promote your team, your company, and the services you offer. Go with that professional goal in mind, get lots of business cards, and show pride in who and what you represent.

The Data Integration Roadmap

If you've reached this point, then congratulations, you're well on your way to having a flourishing integration team. The training classes and online videos are coming fast and furious, you have eager stakeholders with projects in mind, and the ETL jobs have never run so well nor been so optimized. So what's next?

In the previous chapter, we discussed the concept of continuous improvement and being able to improve our existing systems through the Plan-Do-Check-Act (PDCA) model. With the support and encouragement of our colleagues, we should be able to see what and where our integration systems are lacking and merge that with the top priorities the organization has in mind for future development. To take a simple example, imagine we have a request to upgrade delivery into the accounts receivable database, add fields to the contacts target system, and capture additional logging from two new data sources. I highlight these tasks in Figure 9-6.

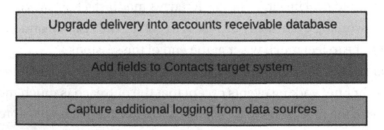

Figure 9-6. *List of Tasks*

---

[20]Lisa Lee, Kim Honjo, and Mark Abramowitz. 2019. Dreamforce '18 by the Numbers." *Salesforce Blog*. www.salesforce.com/blog/2018/10/dreamforce-18-by-the-numbers.html

Right off the bat, we may be inclined to take the easiest one of these tasks and work on this first. But which one is it? Of course, we'd have to have a business analyst deep dive, talk with resources, and communicate the level of effort with developers. Even then, our calculations could be off a bit, and we would start working on one task, only to have a significant issue crop up with one of the other tasks, forcing us to drop our current task mid-development and then jump onto the next fire. Working on that one would do us no good in the long run as the first issue might be begging for our attention, and again, we'd have to shift effort, all the while ignoring the third task with project leads increasingly growing frustrated at our lack of concern.

You can see the problem here. It's not that we don't have the work—we have lots of it—but that we don't have the prioritization of the work. We took a subjective measure of what was the most comfortable to perform first and worked on it until a showstopping interruption occurred. Then we dropped what we were doing and set our priorities on that new issue until other stakeholders chimed in and we refocused back to the original problem. Of course, stakeholders should be able to allocate our priorities, but we can't be all things to all people if our attention and (limited) resources are always in high demand.

To bring normalcy to the chaos, we must strategize and determine what is our highest priority from an organizational standpoint. That is, regardless of the level of effort, what matters most to the accounts receivable team, or whether a system error brings down the contacts database, we must follow an integration roadmap, a strategic plan that communicates the short- and long-term integration system initiatives.[21]

Once we know what matters to the organization, knowing what to prioritize in terms of our next steps becomes more natural. Taking the earlier example, let's say that the CEO announces at the company all-hands that the most crucial goal for the upcoming fiscal year is to ensure that service representatives improve their relationships with customers. Also important, but to a somewhat lesser degree, is for the Finance team to collect payments on time.

If we return to our tasks from Figure 9-6, you can see how we can prioritize this. Ask yourself, based on your new organizational input, what we should be focusing on first, second, third, fourth, and so on. For example, we can take the top corporate priority "Improve relationships with customers" and decide that the most closely related integration task is "Add fields to the contacts target system." The second priority,

[21]"What Is an IT Roadmap? | Benefits and Roadmap Examples." 2019. Productplan.com. www.productplan.com/what-is-an-it-roadmap/

"Financial teams collect payments on time," aligns very well with "Upgrade delivery into accounts receivable database." That leaves our final task, "Capture additional logging from data sources," as the lowest-level task on our list. Figure 9-7 shows our reprioritized task list.

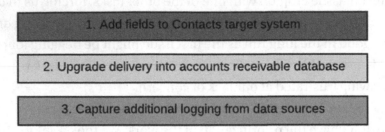

1. Add fields to Contacts target system

2. Upgrade delivery into accounts receivable database

3. Capture additional logging from data sources

Figure 9-7. *List of Tasks, Reprioritized*

We're not done yet. We now know the order of the activities on which we should be working, and we will do that. But we still need to reach out to teams and ask the question: How long? How long will the first task take? How long will the second? The third? And so on.

It's important to stress that we're looking for an overall estimate, not the deep-dive understanding we previously attempted. Although we would like to be as accurate as possible, things inevitably happen, and the time will slip. Plus, there actually could be one or two critical fires that demand our attention, diverting us from the tasks for a brief time, but not enough to throw us off balance. What's essential in our first pass of the roadmap is not the timing of *when*, but the order of *what*.

Let's say we estimate that the time to complete the contacts target system is two months, the upgrade to accounts receivable is one month, and the capture additional logging task is 15 days. Assuming we start on October 1 (the beginning of the fiscal year), we can add a timeline to our model, and our integration roadmap now looks like Figure 9-8.

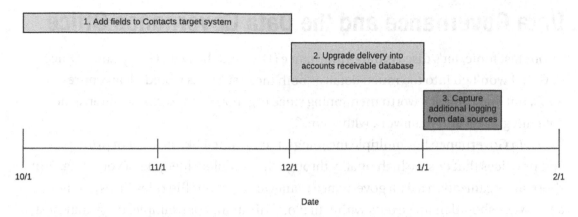

Figure 9-8. *Prioritized Tasks and Time (Our Integration Roadmap)*

Note   In many roadmaps with an agile model, we measure the timeline in terms of sprints. From our simple example, we can easily communicate the direction our team is going and the plan we have in mind. The best part is that we can justify our decisions based on the enterprise list of priorities and collaborate with our colleagues who own the source and target systems to let them know where in the queue we will address their tasks. Although we will not set these delivery dates in stone, they will make our shortlist, and as we've mentioned earlier, making the plan is half the battle.

You may realize now why we saved discussing the roadmap for the end of our chapter on marketing. You must have your integration team and the processes in place, you must have the list of prioritized steps that your stakeholders can provide, and you must have C-level management recognize why your approach matters to the company as a whole. Otherwise, a sustainable roadmap will never come to fruition, and the team remains relegated to maintenance, patches, and the occasional upgrade. Only by reaching outward and getting the full support of the enterprise does actual expansion occur.

Data Governance and the Data Governance Office

As our last topic, let's discuss data governance (DG) and the Data Governance Office (DGO). I won't go into too much detail as both these subjects would fill an entire book, but I do think it's worth mentioning since organizations so closely intertwine data integration and teamwork with them.[22]

Data Governance has multiple meanings, but the one I like is "a set of principles and practices that ensure high quality through the complete lifecycle of your data."[23] In short, an organization's data governance framework lays out the rules (laws) for how employees should manage data within that organization. For example, there may be a specific time that service accounts can go and manipulate data in Production. Anything outside that time is forbidden. Or viewing Personally Identifiable Information (PII) such as credit card numbers is off-limits. Of course, any violation of these rules is subject to punitive action, including suspension and termination.

The benefits of proper data governance are many, but in the world of integration, it means cleaner data, better analytics, better reports, and better decisions. Not having data governance in an organization is like not having a sheriff in an Old West town: you can do it if everyone behaves. Once the gunfighters show up, all bets are off.[24]

Although creating a data governance framework may be easy to understand, putting it into practice is much more difficult. For one, many companies do not have the technology in place or lack the data "maturity" to reach a state where the data can be appropriately governed (see the DMM from Chapter 8). Second, data governance may sound like an IT initiative since, after all, IT teams are usually the ones who manipulate the data, but it requires many departments to agree to its principles. Management, finance, sales, procurement, and legal are just some of the groups that need to safeguard the in-house data and, therefore, must have a say in processes associated with

---

[22]There are a few good DG books I could recommend, but one of my favorites (perhaps outdated by now) was Ladley, John. 2012. *Data Governance*. Waltham, MA: Morgan Kaufmann.

[23]"Data Governance—What, Why, How, Who & 15 Best Practices." 2019. *Enterprise Master Data Management.Profisee*. https://profisee.com/data-governance-what-why-how-who/

[24]There are a few good movies I could recommend, but here's the classic review (never outdated): *High Noon* (1952). 2019. *Imdb*. www.imdb.com/title/tt0044706/?ref_=fn_al_tt_1

ownership, accessibility, security, quality, and knowledge (see Figure 9-9). Achieving their routine consensus and then ensuring teams remain compliant are just two of the many issues that challenge proper data governance.

Figure 9-9. *Data Governance Global View*[25]

Rather than let the data rules run wild, organizations have established a Data Governance Office (DGO), an internal group that defines how to effectively use data resources. The DGO members interpret the use of the governance framework and data management, the actions to take against individuals who violate them, and the peers in their departments to consult when questions or concerns about this data arise.

The DGO is one of the more cutting-edge departments in an organization, but also critical for helping the integration team collaborate and define their role with others. Many potential violations on source system usage or transformation business rules that would usually take weeks to resolve are settled quickly by action from the DGO. For that reason, they make the ultimate contribution in promoting good integration data governance and should be one of the first groups consulted when deciding your roadmap priorities and determining how best to handle the data.

---

[25]"What Is Data Governance | Imperva." 2019. *Learning Center.* www.imperva.com/learn/data-security/data-governance/

Summary

We've reached the end of this chapter and—surprise, surprise—the end of this book. And where are you now? You have your alliances and supporters within and outside the organization, a roadmap for the future, and a coordinated data governance policy with DGO representation. Getting there was tough, but the hardest parts should now be behind you. There's probably a laundry list of next steps you'll want to take to expand even further, but the tools you need to make this happen are already within your grasp. You have a team, a process, a plan, and, perhaps most importantly, enough time in your day to establish realistic timelines with few surprises and even fewer disappointments.

All that you encounter next will be a significant change from where you first started. You have most, if not all, of the recipes and steps you need to be successful with your integration projects, and where you decide to go next is up to you. The next time a project manager approaches you, claiming that all your team needs to do for migration is "push a few buttons" over a weekend, you'll know how to formulate the plan that will make order out of the swirl that is data integration. Now it's time to get out there and to build that team. I wish you all the best.

APPENDIX A

Data Migration Strategy Plan

The Data Migration Strategy Plan outlines the high-level approach for the migration (or integration) portion of the project. It includes the overall project background, required tasks, project assumptions and constraints, current and future state architectures, and other relevant details that will communicate the proposed approach to the reader. To create your first draft, populate each category using the provided guidelines and then add, modify, or delete where necessary.

Overview

[This section introduces the background of the project, usually copied from the proposal or other project management plans. This section also should contain at least one or two paragraphs on the goals of the current migration/integration tasks and how it meets the overall business objectives.]

Introduction

[State the overall vision of the project. You can reference any existing Statements of Work or other artifacts, keeping in mind that a broad definition is supported.]

Purpose

[Describe the purpose of the integration part of the project.]

© Jarrett Goldfedder 2020
J. Goldfedder, *Building a Data Integration Team*, https://doi.org/10.1007/978-1-4842-5653-4

References

[Describe documents that have been used in previous systems or for referencing more project details.]

Assumptions, Constraints, Risks, and Gaps

[This section sets the expectations for the limits of the current project. It defines assumptions (what the team can and cannot do versus what other teams must do), constraints (limitations due to technology or time), risks (potential issues that might occur), and gaps (areas that remain open for debate).]

Assumptions

[Describe any assumptions or dependencies regarding the data conversion effort. These may concern such issues as related software or hardware, operating systems, end user characteristics, and the data that must be available for the conversion.]

Constraints

[Describe any limitations or constraints that have a significant impact on the data conversion effort. Such constraints may be imposed by any of the following (the list is not exhaustive):

- Hardware or software environment
- End user environment (e.g., user work and delivery schedules, timeframes for reports, etc.)
- Availability of resources
- Interoperability requirements (e.g., the order that each system involved in the conversion processes data)
- Interface/protocol requirements

- Data repository and distribution requirements (e.g., volume considerations, such as the size of the database and amount of data to be converted; the number of reads; and the time required for conversions)

- Referential data integrity

- The time allowed to complete the conversion process

- Security requirements]

Risks

[Describe any risks associated with the data conversion and proposed mitigation strategies. Include any risks that could affect conversion feasibility, technical performance of the converted system, the conversion schedule, costs, backup and recovery procedures, etc.]

Gaps

[Describe those parts of the current implementation that are gaps.]

Architecture

[This section contains two broad constructs: the current state and the future state. The current state represents the "as-is" system, that is, where the data currently rests, the data systems involved, the counts of records stored, and other details.

The future state is the "to-be" system—the final snapshot where the data will exist after the project is complete. These subcategories would include parallel topics to the current state, but with more assumptions—most of which is unknown at the outset but will be completed over time.]

Current State

[This diagram will show the current state of the system with all feeders, nodes, and so on. Feel free to use the modeling tool of your choice to represent the way you want the system to look.]

Current State Data Sources

[List the data sources, their description, and the tool/technology used to house and manipulate the data in the existing architecture.]

Current State Record Counts

[Provide the record counts for each relevant entity currently in the source systems. Separate each system into individual tables.]

Current State Data Model

[Describe the high-level data model for the current state (if one exists).]

Current State Integration Points

[List the "integration points"—how the current source-to-target systems are populated in daily loads—which include the source system name, target system name, description of the process, the entities touched (i.e., subject area), the type of integration, the frequency of the occurrence, and (optionally) the number of files required to produce this integration.]

Future State

[Represent the proposed architecture with the data design model, generally produced following initial requirements gathering and consultation with other teams.]

Future State Data Sources

[List the data sources and their description used to house and manipulate the data in future architectures.]

Future State Data Model

[Describe the high-level data model for the future state (if one exists).]

Future State Integration Points

[List how the future source-to-target systems populate in daily loads—which includes the interface (target) name, the ETL direction (inbound outbound), the source system, the target system, the description of the process, the entities touched (i.e., subject area), and the data format.]

Development Tools

[Describe the tools for development, including your ETL tools, scripting languages, or any other technology. We've discussed several of them in Chapter 7. Additional tools/ technologies could include ETL tools such as Informatica, Pentaho, Data Loader, Cast Iron, Jitterbit, and so on.]

Environment Usage

[Describe the different environments that support the implementation, such as Development, Test, and Production—see Chapter 7 for more details.]

Data Migration Approach

[This section covers the overall approach to the integration, such as scope; roles and responsibilities of team members; what should take place pre-, during, and post-migration; and contingency plans. It also describes how data will move from the source to the target and supplemental systems.]

Scope

[Defines the scope of data migration/integration such as quantity and history, as well as those items NOT included in migration such as data profiling or data remediation.]

Approach

[Defines how the data migration will take place using the source systems, the ETL tool, and the environments. This section is the general, as opposed to the detailed plan covered in the Data Migration Process Flow Design.]

Team Roles and Responsibilities

[Defines the names and titles of stakeholders involved with the overall migration strategy and their roles.]

Migration Process

[Introduces the migration process where you describe what will happen during the steps of pre-migration, during migration, and post-migration. It is generally an introduction to the parts that come next.]

Pre-migration Activities

[Defines the major pre-migration activities such as preparing the data loads through profiling and remediation, acquiring login access to systems, and loading sample data.]

Migration Activities

[Define the major migration activities from preparation to test to deployment, including the high-level mapping of objects between source and target. The detailed step-by-step review is described in the Data Migration Process Flow plan.]

Post-Migration Activities

[Defines the major post-migration activities such as monitoring (see Chapter 8), operations and maintenance, and future design reviews.]

Contingency Plan

[Defines the contingency plan should the deploy fails and rollback or reiteration is necessary.]

Testing/Validation

[Describes the framework for the type of tests we plan to conduct, such as unit testing, joint integration, verification testing, and so on. It also describes the testing environment and which of our project teams will be in charge of the tests.]

Testing Methods

[Describes the methods of testing we plan to conduct (unit testing, joint integration, blue-green), as well as the measurements provided to confirm the testing such as inputs, outputs, and definitions of success.]

Migration

[Describes the tests conducted to confirm migration success/failure.]

Integration

[Describes the tests conducted to confirm integration success/failure.]

APPENDIX B

Data Profiling Template

All data should be identified within the source systems to understand the shape, consistency, and variability among the individual records. The goal of the integration team is to gather the systems, tables, fields, and other source inputs and then analyze each of these records either from the source or through input staging files. Although every project migration is different, data usually has a specific pattern that is worth noting in a data profiling document. Don McMunn (www.ipcdesigns.com/data_profiling/) has provided a data profiling tool that can aid in this effort. See Table B-1 for several of the fields that I have found the most useful along with an Excel spreadsheet (located at *https://github.com/Apress/building-a-data-integration-team/tree/master/templates*) with several samples to get you started.

Table B-1. *Description of Profiling Fields*

Field	Description
TNAME	Name of table containing column being profiled
CNAME	Name of column in table being profiled
DATA_TYPE	Name of the data type of the column
DATA_LENGTH	Maximum length of the column in bytes
NUM_TABLE_ROWS	Total number of rows contained in the table at the time of the data profiling pass
NUM_DISTINCT_VALUES	Total number of unique values found in the column at the time of the data profiling pass
MIN_DATA_LENGTH	Shortest length of data value found in this column; mainly useful for string data types

(continued)

215

© Jarrett Goldfedder 2020
J. Goldfedder, *Building a Data Integration Team*, https://doi.org/10.1007/978-1-4842-5653-4

Table B-1. (*continued*)

Field	Description
MAX_DATA_LENGTH	Longest length of data value found in this column; mainly useful for string data types
NUM_NULLS	Total number of NULL values found in the column at the time of the data profiling pass
DENSITY	A ratio of non-null values to total rows in the table
ALPHANUM_COUNT	Number of rows containing ONLY an alphanumeric value that is not either a date or a numeric-only value
DATE_COUNT	Number of rows containing ONLY a valid date value in this column
NUMERIC_COUNT	Number of rows containing ONLY numeric values in this column regardless of data type
MIN_ALPHANUM_VALUE	Minimum alphanumeric value found in a string column; based on default page
MAX_ALPHANUM_VALUE	Maximum alphanumeric value found in a string column; based on default page
MIN_NUMERIC_VALUE	Smallest numeric value found in a numeric column
MAX_NUMERIC_VALUE	Largest numeric value found in a numeric column
MIN_DATE_VALUE	Oldest date value found in this column
MAX_DATE_VALUE	Most recent data found in this date column
NUM_EMAIL_INVALID	(If field is an EMAIL field) How many of these records are invalid?
NUM_CONTAINS_ NONASCII	How many records contain characters outside the range of normal ASCII values (i.e., foreign and non-printable values such as ä or line feeds ^013)?
PICKLIST_VALUE	(If field is a PICKLIST field) What are the values?

APPENDIX C

Issues Log Template

The Issues Log template is designed to record and track any issues or questions related to data quality and data migration follow-up. This document is similar in purpose to other software-based issues logs in that it anticipates requirement follow-ups or potential data corrections. In any case, it is convenient to have for documenting bugs and moving the project forward if data product owners are limited in availability.

I provide some basic Issues Log fields with associated definitions in Table C-1.

Table C-1. *Issues Log Tracking Fields and Definitions*

Field	Definition
Project Name	The name of the project under review
Date of Document	The current log publication date
Issue	This value should be a standard numbering system (e.g., 001, 002, 003)
Description	A detailed description of the issue
Priority	High, medium, or low priority
Category	Assign to a category
Reported By	Who reported the issue?
Assigned To	To whom is the issue assigned?
Status	What is the status of the issue?
Date Resolved	What date was the issue resolved?
Resolution/Comments	What was the resolution, or what is being done to resolve the issue?

© Jarrett Goldfedder 2020
J. Goldfedder, *Building a Data Integration Team*, https://doi.org/10.1007/978-1-4842-5653-4

APPENDIX D

Source-to-Target Mapping Template

As the name implies, the Source-to-Target Mapping template maps the association of data from the source to target systems. This spreadsheet is referenced and modified throughout the requirements gathering, build, testing, and monitoring phases, perhaps serving as the most important deliverable for the team. Consequently, the goal of the Source-to-Target Mapping spreadsheet should be to supply enough transformation rules and technical decisions to readers without overwhelming them with details.

A quick Internet search will reveal many recommendations for the "best" Source-to-Target mapping template. I have identified in Table D-1 the fields and associated definitions that have served me well for the majority of my projects, but yours may differ. Feel free to modify, add, or subtract where necessary, keeping in mind that we want to balance flexibility with comprehension and not go too far in either direction.

219

© Jarrett Goldfedder 2020
J. Goldfedder, *Building a Data Integration Team*, https://doi.org/10.1007/978-1-4842-5653-4

Table D-1. *Source-to-Target Mapping Fields and Definitions*

Field	Definition
SourceDatasystem	Put the formal name for the system that is the data source, for example, "Mailing List," "Recruiting"
SourceTable	The physical name of the source table, for example, "CONTACT,""PRODUCT"
SourceField	The physical name of the source field/column, for example, "ROWID," "FIRSTNAME"
SourceDataType	The data type for the source data, for example, "VARCHAR(30)," "DATETIME(mm/dd/yyyy)," "NUMBER"
TargetDatasystem	Put the formal name for the system that is the data target, for example, "Salesforce," "DataWarehouse"
TargetTable	The physical name of the target table, for example, "MERCHANDISE__C,""ACCOUNT"
TargetField	The physical name of the target field/column, for example, "ROWID," "FIRSTNAME"
TargetDataType	The data type for the target data, for example, "STRING," "REFERENCE," "NUMBER"
TransformationRule	Enter the high-level business rules required for transforming the data from source to target, for example, "Join constituent.contact_id on constituent_add.rowid where address.primary_address = TRUE and address.valid=TRUE"
PicklistValues	Insert related picklist values, especially if customized, for example, "Freshman, Sophomore, Junior, Senior," "Small, Medium, Large"
DesignNotes	Use this field to provide additional design notes that are not necessarily part of the transformation rules, for example, "Values for this field are not case sensitive and should be reviewed before import," "Trim those values that exceed the maximum datatype for this field"
DateCreated	Insert the initial date this field was added to the model, for example, "12/1/2019"

(*continued*)

Table D-1. (*continued*)

Field	Definition
DateLastUpdated	Insert the date this field mapping was modified, for example, "12/22/2019"
OpenIssues	Insert any open issues encountered during development, for example, "We are missing several row identifiers in the join," "What should we do with fields that go over 80 characters?"
Assumption	Describe the workaround/assumption for the open issues, for example, "Ignore all joins where the ID does not match," "Trim fields at 80 characters"
AssumptionApproved	List whether the assumption was approved and who approved it. If NOT approved, list the workaround specified. For example: "Assumption approved by J. Smith," "Workaround should be to omit all records where field > 80 characters--S. Brown"
ResolutionCloseDate	Insert the date the resolution was deemed as closed, for example, "12/08/2019"
FollowUpRequired	Indicate whether this data needs follow-up. During a filter, this will help guide conversations. For example: "YES," "NO"

APPENDIX E

Data Migration Process Flow Design Template

The Data Migration Process Flow provides a detailed design for migration processes, including the order of operations. It can be considered a technical appendix to the Data Migration Strategy, intended to provide the step-by-step processes that fulfill the proposal offered in that document. This document tracks the migration at a granular level and, therefore, should be updated and reviewed after each change in scope to ensure the requirements still are in alignment with stakeholder expectations.

Order of Operation

[Describe the step-by-step operation for object migration. For example:]

This document defines the process flow for development, deployment, and cleanup required to migrate the stakeholder's list of data. These activities can vary in time, depending on the volume of data provided and the complexity of updates.

The integration team presents the breakdown for deployment to Development, Test, and Production environments in Figure E-1. These individual steps performed for each task are summarized later in this document.

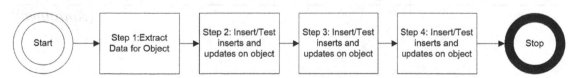

Figure E-1. *Sample Project Flow*

J. Goldfedder, *Building a Data Integration Team*, https://doi.org/10.1007/978-1-4842-5653-4

Mapping Logic

[This section defines the high-level rules for migrating source-to-target data, mostly used to confirm with the client that these migrations are accurate. You will be referencing your Source-to-Target Mapping spreadsheet at some point in this section. As indicated throughout this book, the spreadsheet should be available in a separate spreadsheet or database, and you can include a summary table for easy reference. For example:]

Due to currently existing duplications as well as priority field determination, the integration team has included business logic as part of the ETL process. In collaboration with stakeholder requirements, the integration team has summarized the business rules for populating the target data store. The following source-to-target maps identify these transformation rules (last column) as well as the source system, the source location (i.e., the database or CSV file containing all deduplicated records), the source field name, and the target object and field. Table E-1 shows the field mapping for the MYCONTACTDB source system to the CONTACT target.

Table E-1. *Field Mappings for the MYCONTACTDB Source System*

Source System	Source Location	Source Field	Target Object	Target Field	Transformation Rule
MYCONTACTDB	Contact_Users	Full_Name	CONTACT	FIRSTNAME	Extract first name from source with following rule: (EXTRACT,Full_Name, " ")
MYCONTACTDB	Contact_Users	Full_Name	CONTACT	MIDDLENAME	Extract first name from source with following rule: (EXTRACT,Full_Name, " ", " ")

(continued)

Table E-1. (*continued*)

Source System	Source Location	Source Field	Target Object	Target Field	Transformation Rule
MYCONTACTDB	Contact_Users	Full_Name	CONTACT	LASTNAME	Extract first name from source with following rule: (EXTRACT FROM RIGHT,Full_Name, " ")
MYCONTACTDB	EMAIL spreadsheet	email	CONTACT	EMAIL	Direct transform action (note: only the first EMAIL value from the EMAIL table will be used; the second value (EMAIL) will be added to CONTACT. Description field)

Deployment Steps

[Define each step of the process that will occur during migration, along with a detailed description. The resulting flowchart should provide context for stakeholders and developers as well as a guide for deployment. Each step should then be summarized in a single sentence. For example, Figure E-2 illustrates the flowchart for analyzing, testing, and deploying Contact records into two distinct environments.]

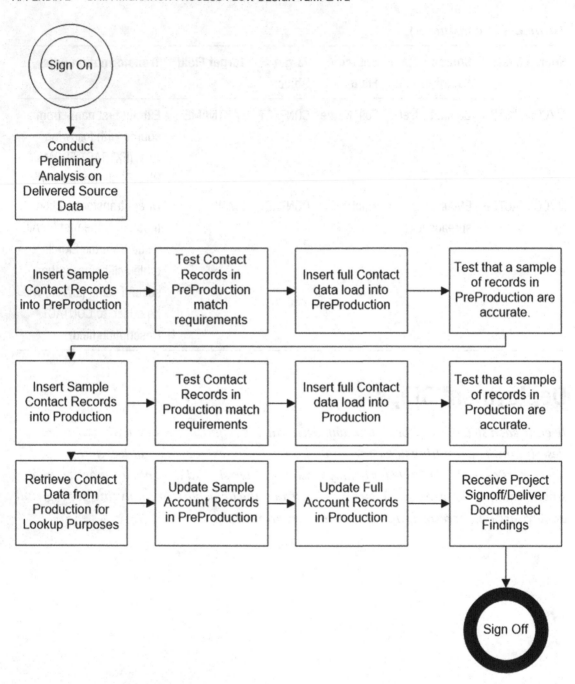

Figure E-2. *Step-By-Step Deployment*

Description of Prerequisites

- Step 0: Receive records for review; evaluate if existing IDs link with existing contact data (based on LEGACY_ID keys). Create lists of updates versus inserts based on found values.

Contact

- Step 1: Insert sample contact records into Preproduction—five to ten sample contact records will bulk load via the Oracle SQL*Loader tool.

- Step 2: QA assessment of five to ten records with feedback followed by reiteration/deletion of sample records/reload (if needed).

- Step 3: Migrate remaining contacts through the Oracle SQL*Loader tool.

- Step 4: Final check of records loaded/send out log files.

- Steps 5–8: Repeat process in the Production environment.

Account

- Step 9: Perform export of CONTACT object stored in Production and import into Staging database for reference lookup.

- Step 10: Update account record sample, followed by QA assessment with feedback (should take no longer than 1 hour).

- Step 11: Update full account load in the Production environment.

Project Signoff/Document Delivery

- During this final phase, the project will receive authorized signoff, and a final document will be placed into Salesforce Content as a reference package.

Log File Delivery

[Indicates where the deployment success and error logs will be stored. For example:]

Individual Delivery

At the end of each stage, log files identifying the individual SUCCESS and ERRORS (i.e., fallout) will be available for review. Oracle SQL∗Loader will provide this file in a log report which team members can reach from the corporate Q:\ drive.

Success and errors counts, as well as load time, will also be tracked separately in spreadsheets to ensure appropriate benchmarking.

Portal Storage

Data logs for all deployments, both test and production, are archived in SharePoint and available for review from `https://corporatesharepointwebsite.com`.

Migration Results

[Once the migration is complete, record the high-level success and error results and any additional notes for each object. For example:]

Contact
Inserts

- # Records Inserted: 200000
- # Successes: 145158
- # Failures: 54842
- Due to field names being incorrect, the majority of errors were for empty Last Name (53,811) and First Name (1,031) fields.

Updates

- # Records Updated: 26,079

- 100% Success

Account

- # New Records Updated: 92192

- # Existing Records Updated: 36

- 100% Success

Final Signoff

[As a final step, prepare an email screenshot from the project sponsor or product owner that the deployment was successful and the target system received the data per requirements. Generally, this signoff happens after deployment and establishes that the right people were satisfied with the deployment results. For example:]

The project sponsor has confirmed that the target data source on 12/22/2019 successfully received Production contact and account data (see Figure E-3), thereby concluding this migration.

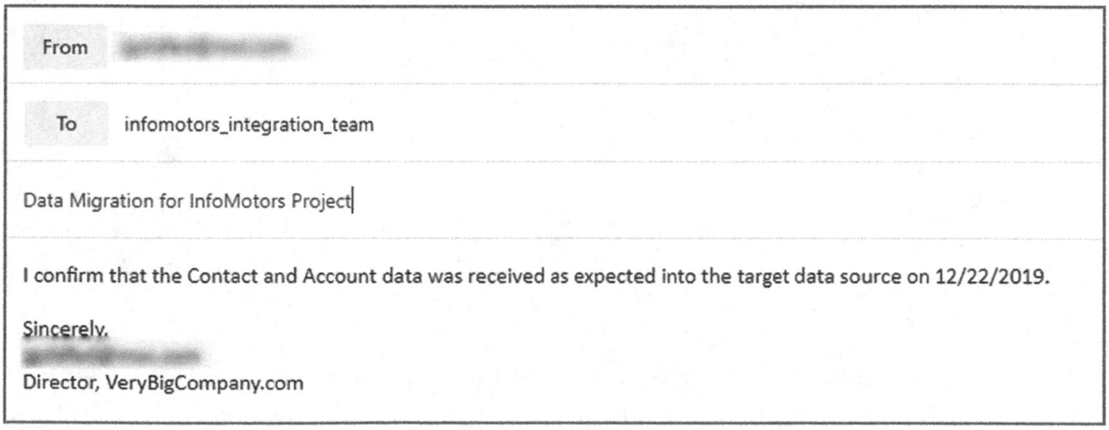

From	
To	infomotors_integration_team

Data Migration for InfoMotors Project

I confirm that the Contact and Account data was received as expected into the target data source on 12/22/2019.

Sincerely,

Director, VeryBigCompany.com

Figure E-3. *Sample Project Flow*

APPENDIX F

Migration Results Report Template

The Migration Results Report template provides the summary statistics for data transfer between source and target systems, grouping by table or object, success/error counts, and action items. The integration team should populate this record after each migration, from development to mock testing to eventual production. These results will enable you to predict deployment times as well as errors that may or may not need resolution. You may want to add your final results to the Migration Results section of the Data Migration Process Flow.

The basic layout is self-explanatory, containing nine fields in total (see Table F-1 for field names, definitions, and an example). As with the other templates available, feel free to make whatever modifications, additions, or subtractions you need to ensure your measurements are repeatable, consistent, and predictable.

Table F-1. *Issues Log Tracking Fields and Definitions*

Field	Definition	Example
Table/Object	The source table or object you are migrating	ACCOUNT
Method	The type of migration you are performing. There are five types available—Query, Delete, Insert, Update, and Upsert (i.e., a combination of Insert and Update) Most of the time, your activity will be either Insert, Update, or Upsert	Insert
Start Date	The date and time that the migration begins execution. Note that this is a TIMESTAMP field that must include hours, minutes, and, if measurable, seconds	4/18/2019 2:19 PM
End Date	The date and time that the migration begins execution. Note that this is a TIMESTAMP field that must include hours, minutes, and, if measurable, seconds	4/18/2016 2:25 PM
Delta Load	A formula field (in minutes or seconds) that subtracts the end date from the start date	6 minutes (360 seconds)
Total Records	The total number of records available for migration	50
Success Count	The number of records successfully transferred from the source object to the target object	47
Error Count	The number of records unsuccessfully transferred from the source object to the target object	3
Error Message	The error messages (separated by semicolons) produced during the migration. If the same error message occurs multiple times, then list that message once followed by the total number of times it appears	"Value too large for column 'MIDDLE INITIAL' (actual: 4, maximum: 1), "Cannot insert NULL into (string)" (2)

Index

A

Agile model, 5–6, 203
Automation
    Execution Results Logging
        pane, 151, 152, 154
    testing
        CSV file, 153
        ETL source csv Error, 154, 155
        test scripts, 152

B

Business Error, 150, 153

C

Command-line interface
    (CLI) tool, 161
Cross-Functional team, 31

D

Data governance (DG), 204
Data Governance
    Office (DGO), 205
Data Management Maturity Model
    (DMM) model
    definition, 180
    maturity levels, 182, 183

Data migration process flow
    design template
    deployment
        account records, 227
        contact records, 227
        example, 225
        prerequisites, 227
    final signoff, 229
    log file delivery, 228
    mapping logic, 224
    migration results, 228
    operations, 223
Data Migration Strategy Plan
    architecture
        current state, 210
        future state, 210
    assumptions, 208
    constraints, 208, 209
    development tools
        environment usage, 211
        migration approach, 211
        migration process, 212
        testing/validation, 212
    risks, 209
Data profiling
    template, 215
Data Transformation
    Services (DTS), 96
Dell Boomi, 92, 93

© Jarrett Goldfedder 2020
J. Goldfedder, *Building a Data Integration Team*, https://doi.org/10.1007/978-1-4842-5653-4

Printed in the United States
By Bookmasters